To:

_____

From:

_____

Date:

_____

HOW TO HEAR THE VOICE OF GOD

HOW TO HEAR THE VOICE OF GOD

GM VISION

The objective of our vision is to spiritually feed God's people through preaching and teaching; and to take the Word of God every where it is needed.

ISBN: 1-59272-091-9

Second Edition 2005

Cover design by:
GM International - Design Department

Editor:
GM International

Category:
Prophecy: How to Hear the Voice of God

Published by:
GM International
13651 SW 143 Ct., #101
Miami, FL 33186
(305) 233-3325 Fax (305) 233-3328

Printed by:
GM International, USA

Printed in Colombia

Dedication

*T*his book is dedicated to our Lord and Savior Jesus Christ who is the only one who deserves the honor, glory and praise; He is the King of kings and Lord of lords. Thank you for giving me life and for being the main reason for my existence.

Acknowledgements

would like to thank God to whom I belong and serve. Thank you for your strength and for your help in my daily walk. I would also like to express my deepest appreciation to my wife and children for their unconditional support and for sharing this ministry with me.

To the leadership, the intercessors and everyone who, in one way or another contributed even in the smallest details, thank you and God bless you!

Index

Index

Prologue

While reading this book, I was reminded of the following Scripture:

"^{25}And there are also many other things that Jesus did, which if they were written one by one, I suppose that even the world itself could not contain the books that would be written. Amen." John 21.25

With this in mind, use your imagination and walk with me into one of the many Christian Bookstores available today. Look around at the thousands of books that have been written about "the Book." More than likely, you will find many versions covering the wide range of topics found in the Bible. With these many options available, is it possible to find a little spiritual gold within this mountain of paper and ink? Many times we are blessed to have God himself place in our hands such a book, worthy of our time and effort. This book is certainly one of those special books written by someone who knows God and not by someone who only knows about God.

The topic "How to Hear the Voice of God" is vitally important. We are living in difficult times and we are in dire need of spiritual ears to hear what He has to say. This book is not full of fat, taking up space throughout its pages. Instead, it is a mountain of spiritual steak for those who love to eat meat.

Although this book is entitled, "How to Hear the Voice of God," in it you will not find the "How to, in ten easy steps" guide. What you will find is the calling to holiness, obedience, faith and spiritual maturity. This is, of course, if you are truly searching for the powerful manifestation of the Holy Spirit to operate in your life.

Careful emphasis has been given to the different ways Jesus reveals Himself through God's power in our lives as we serve Him. Each line is full of detailed instructions, definitions, applications and easy examples of daily living.

A gift, which is manifested in a teacher, consists in taking a difficult subject and presenting it in an easy to understand format. Not trying to impress the reader with his wisdom but in showing his earnest desire to teach and to edify the body of Christ. The ability to understand and to apply the information received when the teaching is over is the true test of a teacher. This book reflects this and much more.

I have three decades of experience in the ministry of the gifts of the Spirit; yet, this book has taught me new things, inspiring me to dig deeper in the things of God and to expect more of Him like never before.

You are holding in your hands an anointed book, but as the author teaches us, "knowledge alone is not enough." You must purpose in your heart to take what you learn and apply it into every area of your life.

Dr. Ronald E. Short
Apostle and Teacher
Evangelistic Missionary to the Hispanic World

Introduction

The greatest limitation for believers is the difficulty to hear God's voice. From the moment of our birth and throughout our lifetime, we become accustomed to hearing the different voices that come from different sources. Because of this, discerning the voice of God becomes an odyssey for many.

The church has the urgent need to know and develop the ability to clearly hear God's voice. This, and the lack of information regarding this subject, inspired me to write this book.

Old beliefs that declare that God only spoke in the past or that the great servants of God are the only privileged people able to hear His voice must change. God wants to communicate with His people today. You must embrace this truth if you truly want to hear the voice of the Holy Spirit.

As you read this book, you will discover many details based on easy to understand biblical truths that will help you recognize God's voice.

CHAPTER I

God Wants to Speak to us

$\mathcal{O}$n this dark, insecure and fearful world in which we live in, and with the many voices surrounding us, it is important for every believer, minister and leader to learn how to hear God's voice. Until now, we have seen the extreme in evangelistic circles in relationship to this topic, such as people not believing that God still speaks to us today. They believe God spoke long ago, but now remains quiet. However, throughout Scripture, it is clear that God always wants to speak and communicate with His people.

On the other hand, we must keep in mind that there are many believers who use the name of God in vain when they say phrases such as: "God said to me," "God says I should get a divorce," "God says you should marry me." Many people use God's name to manipulate, control and do things that go against His will, but in truth, God has never spoken to them. God hates the sin of lying and taking His name in vain. To declare something as if He said it, results in grave consequences, and according to the following verse, it brings curses into our lives.

"⁷You shall not take the name of the LORD your God in vain, for the LORD will not hold him guiltless who takes His name in vain." Exodus 20.7

Though many people use the name of God in vain, it does not mean there aren't people who genuinely hear God's voice and speak what He says. The purpose of this book is to teach you how to hear the voice of God and to teach others to do the same.

We are the result of our own decisions. For this reason, it is imperative to recognize that our decisions today affect what we will become tomorrow. We can't afford to make decisions based on past experiences or someone else's opinions. We must learn to hear the voice of God, seek His face and be careful not to make any rash decisions. *We need to learn how to hear the voice of God!*

Does God speak today?

As previously mentioned, many people hold fast to old patterns of thought based on past experiences which shaped their belief that God no longer speaks to His people. The Word of God teaches that God spoke yesterday, speaks today and will continue to speak to us. This demonstrates His desire to communicate with His people.

"¹God, who at various times and in various ways spoke in time past to the fathers by the prophets, ²has in these last days spoken to us by His Son, whom He has appointed heir of all things, through whom also He made the worlds." Hebrews 1.1, 2

Let us take a look at a few biblical examples where God spoke to people who knew how to hear His voice.

In the Old Testament...

• God spoke to Moses.

   The Word of God teaches that God spoke to Moses face to face. There was no need for an intermediary.

"14And God said to Moses, 'I AM WHO I AM.' And He said, 'Thus you shall say to the children of Israel, I AM has sent me to you.'" Exodus 3.14

- God spoke to Samuel.

God spoke to Samuel in an audible voice. His response was that of obedience.

"10Now the LORD came and stood and called as at other times, Samuel! Samuel! And Samuel answered, 'Speak, for Your servant hears.'" 1 Samuel 3.10

In the New Testament...

- God spoke to the Apostle Paul.

During the time when the Apostle Paul persecuted the church and its believers, using letters giving him permission for it, the Lord appeared to him in a vision and spoke:

"3As he journeyed he came near Damascus, and suddenly a light shone around him from heaven. 4Then he fell to the ground, and heard a voice saying to him, 'Saul, Saul, why are you persecuting Me?'" Acts 9.3, 4

- God spoke to the Apostle John.

John continued to seek the Lord wholeheartedly during his imprisonment in the Isle of Patmos. Through the Scriptures we learn that God spoke to him revealing the Book of Revelation.

"10I was in the Spirit on the Lord's Day, and I heard behind me a loud voice, as of a trumpet." Revelation 1.10

It is clear that God's desire is to speak to His people, not only in the past, but also in the present. God is real and He lives. We must begin to change our old way of thinking that says God only speaks to certain people.

Why does God want to speak to you?

There is one reason why God wants to speak to you:

God's desire is to communicate His plans and purpose for your life.

Communication is part of who He is. It is God's nature to speak to His creation. He communicates His desires and plans. He confirms the past and tells us about our present and future, because it is an intricate part of who He is.

Scripture speaks to you; it says, *"...if you hear His voice today..."* It is teaching you that He is still talking. God abides in the eternal present; this is why His name is the Great I Am. God is today, in other words, God still speaks and heals you today. If you are willing to obey Him, you will hear His voice. Perhaps, at times, your spiritual ears may be "obstructed" making it difficult for you to hear His voice when He speaks, but the Word of God teaches that He is Spirit. Therefore, to hear His voice, you must also live in the Spirit.

In the Old Testament, God spoke to the prophets, kings and priests. When the people needed to hear from Him, they had to seek the counsel of the prophet for an answer from God. In the New Testament, God renews your spirit making it easy for you to hear directly from Him. God might still choose to use a prophet to speak to you, but He will also speak directly into your spirit.

The moment that Adam committed the first sin humanity lost the ability to hear God's voice. Darkness filled his spirit. Later, Jesus was born, crucified, and on the third day, He was raised from the dead. His sacrifice was necessary to restore humanity from sin. Now those who choose to believe in Him are born again and enjoy eternal life.

The new birth brings several things into the spirit of man:

"²⁵Then I will sprinkle clean water on you, and you shall be clean; I will cleanse you from all your filthiness and from all your idols. ²⁶I will give you a new heart and put a new spirit within you; I will take the heart of stone out of your flesh and give you a heart of flesh. ²⁷I will put My Spirit within you and cause you to walk in My statutes and you will keep My judgments and do them." Ezekiel 36.25-27

- **A new spirit or heart.** In the new birth, a complete renovation takes place in your heart; it gives you the ability to hear God's voice once more, as Adam did, when he walked in the Garden of Eden.

- **The Holy Spirit dwells within you.** Once the blood of Jesus cleanses and changes you, God comes to live in you. The Word of God teaches that you are the Temple of the Holy Spirit.

- **A heart of flesh.** God changes your heart, making it sensitive to His voice and to His leading. Sinners can't hear God's voice because their spirit and conscience are anesthetized by sin, but born again believers have the ability to hear the Lord.

- **A heart that is able to hear, to understand and to obey His Word.** When these things come to pass, your spirit is ready to walk in the supernatural. Your spirit is renewed and restored through the new birth. Every new believer is able to hear God's voice and walk in the supernatural.

Man is a three-part being.

When we refer to man as a three-part being, we are saying that man is divided into three parts: body, soul and spirit.

Spirit – you communicate with God through your born-again spirit because He is Spirit.

"23 But the hour is coming, and now is, when the true worshipers will worship the Father in spirit and truth; for the Father is seeking such to worship Him. 24 God is Spirit and those who worship Him must worship in spirit and truth."
John 4.23, 24

This passage declares that God speaks and communicates with man through man's renewed spirit. What a wonderful revelation: the fact that you can speak with your Father face to face as He shares with you His plans and purpose.

Soul – this is where the thoughts and emotions of man reside. God communicates to man through his spirit, not his soul.

Body – the spirit and soul of man are in the body. God does not speak through your body, either.

Man communicates with God through man's renewed spirit.

What are the three great voices in the world?

In a darkened and fearful world, it is imperative to learn how to discern these three voices and to make wise decisions based only on God's voice.

1. **The voice of your spirit.** The Word of God calls this voice your conscience. It is part of your spirit and it teaches you to discern between good and evil.

"16This being so, I myself always strive to have a conscience without offense toward God and men." Acts 24.16

2. **The voice of the devil.** The devil speaks to you in the same way God speaks to His people. He tries to imitate God's voice, hoping to deceive you. I have witnessed how the enemy deceives believers because they never learned how to discern the different voices.

3. **The voice of God.** God speaks to you in many ways. One is through the Holy Spirit. Whenever the Holy Spirit speaks to you, it's because God wants to communicate something of extreme importance. It may have something to do with life, death, a call to ministry or perhaps a great revelation for His kingdom.

How can you discern these voices?

I have been asked the following question many times: "Pastor, how do I know when God is speaking to me, or if it's the devil's voice, or just my own spirit speaking to me?" This usually happens when a believer is not familiarized with God's voice. The following illustration will make this clear.

There are different types of radio frequencies needed to capture the various radio waves in the air: SW, AM, FM and FM stereo.

- **SW or short wave radio.** This radio wave has a lot of interference. Because of this, a special antenna is needed to receive it and to hear it more clearly than with AM radio waves. For the most part, short wave frequencies are used for long distance communication, thus making it difficult to hear with clarity.

- **AM frequency.** Generally speaking, this airwave has little or no interference at night, but it is still unclear at times.

- **FM frequency.** This airwave is much clearer and crisp than the others. However, it may, at times, experience some light interference or noise.

- **FM stereo frequency.** This airwave frequency is by far the clearest. It gives you clear, crisp sound. The reception on FM stereo is exceptional. It is so good it might give the impression that the person speaking is standing right next to you. There is no interference in this frequency.

Just as there are different levels of frequency in radio waves, there are many believers able to hear the voice of God in different frequencies. Some are unable to hear Him clearly, while others hear His voice, but experience light interference. Then there are believers who know how to hear God's voice clearly.

What spiritual exercises should you practice to improve your ability to hear God's voice?

- **Fasting and prayer.** Fasting makes your spirit sensitive to God's voice.

- **Praying abundantly in the spirit.** When you pray in other tongues, your spirit is edified and developed. Make it a point to pray in the spirit or in other tongues for one hour every day. After six months you will see something begin to happen within your spirit, you will become sensitive to God's voice.

- **Meditating on the Word of God.** When you meditate on the Word of God, you become sensitive to His voice. Choose a verse from the Bible every day. Meditate on its words; declare them; think about them all day long. Soon you will begin to see the results.

Knowing to discern these three voices depends on:

- **Spiritual maturity.** A sign of spiritual maturity is when the believer is guided by the Holy Spirit to act upon something. The mature believer learns to discern, and to know the voice of God.

"¹⁴For as many as are led by the Spirit of God, these are sons of God." Romans 8.14

- **Practicing how to discern God's voice.** When you continually use your senses to hear God's voice you will learn to discern when He is talking to you or when it is another voice. Discerning God's voice and learning to operate in your spiritual gifts is a process that is developed through practice.

"14But solid food belongs to those who are of full age, that is, those who by reason of use have their senses exercised to discern both good and evil." Hebrews 5.14

As you practice listening to God's voice, you will grow and become familiarized with it. Eventually, you will reach the point of being able to say, as Jesus said in John 10.27, *"27My sheep hear My voice, and I know them, and they follow Me."* Listening to the voice of God is an exercise you must do continually in order to develop the ability to discern His voice, among other voices. Man was exclusively created to hear God's voice. Because of this, it should be easy for every believer to hear His voice all the time.

What is the fundamental key to hearing God's voice?

* Your willingness to obey.

One reason God stops talking to believers is because of their disobedience when He speaks. Many believers approach me with the following declaration, "Pastor, God doesn't speak to me." Before you say this, ask yourself when was the last time God spoke the word and you didn't obey? If this statement is true about you, repent. God will speak to you again. He speaks when you choose to obey.

The word "obedience" implies two things in the Greek language: *"Akouo,"* meaning to hear and obey; and the word *"hupakouo,"* meaning to persuade, to listen and to hear with the intention to obey. In essence, obedience means to hear with spiritual ears and to practice what God commands.

Sometimes God will ask you to do things that go against all reasoning. Perhaps what He asks will be difficult to do, but you have to be willing to obey regardless of where you are; what circumstances you may find yourselves in; or who is around you. If your desire is to hear His voice, obedience is the key to achieving this goal. Personally, I prefer to be wrong thinking I am obeying God than to be wrong by doing nothing at all.

CHAPTER II

Methods and Means by Which God Speaks

$\mathcal{O}$ n the previous chapter you learned that God desires to speak to you through your renewed spirit and the fundamental reasons why He desires to do it. It is His nature to want to communicate to you His plans and purpose.

Now you will study the means through which God reveals himself to His people and how He communicates with you. There are three ways through which we perceive Him:

- **Hearing**

  Hearing implies to hear spiritually, not physically. Your spirit has a spiritual ear just as your body has a physical ear. Listening with your spiritual ears is one way God speaks to you.

  "13 So it was, when Elijah heard it, that he wrapped his face in his mantle and went out and stood in the entrance of the cave. Suddenly a voice came to him, and said, 'What are you doing here, Elijah?'" 1 Kings 19.13

- **Seeing**

  Seeing in the spirit means that the Lord is allowing you to see into the spiritual realm. When this happens, you are able to see mental images, visions and dreams.

"⁴⁷Jesus saw Nathanael coming toward Him, and said of him, 'Behold, an Israelite indeed, in whom is no deceit!' ⁴⁸Nathanael said to Him, 'How do You know me?' Jesus answered and said to him, 'Before Philip called you, when you were under the fig tree, I saw you'." John 1.47, 48

- **Feeling**

Feeling is a perception, an intuition of the Holy Spirit within you; it is not knowledge having to do with the physical or carnal senses, but a testimony, an impression within your spirit.

"²³...except that the Holy Spirit testifies in every city, saying that chains and tribulations await me. ²⁴But none of these things move me; nor do I count my life dear to myself, so that I may finish my race with joy, and the ministry which I received from the Lord Jesus, to testify to the gospel of the grace of God." Acts 20.23, 24

Believers should familiarize themselves with the way God speaks to them. As for me, God usually speaks to me through impressions and sight, but God speaks to believers in different ways.

How can you be sure it is His voice you hear?

It is impossible to recognize a counterfeit one hundred-dollar bill if you have never seen the real thing. The counterfeit bill can only be detected if you are familiar with the real thing. This same principle can be applied when you know God's voice. It is easy to identify the voice of the enemy because you are familiar with the voice of God.

"³To him the doorkeeper opens, and the sheep hear his voice; and he calls his own sheep by name and leads them out. ⁴And when he brings out his own sheep, he goes before them; and the sheep follow him, for they know his voice. ⁵Yet they will by no means follow a stranger, but will flee from him, for they do not know the voice of strangers." John 10.3-5

What methods does God use to speak to you?

The means through which God speaks to you is through hearing, seeing and feeling. Now you will study the **methods** He uses to speak to you. The first method God uses to speak to you is the inner witness.

1. The inner witness

What is the inner witness? It is an impression within your spirit, an intuition, a perception, an understanding; it is a feeling and an impulse in your spirit.

Intuition resides within your spirit. It helps you to understand and to perceive all things in the spirit. The testimony within you is not a voice, but a feeling, a small impression, an understanding in your spirit given by the Holy Spirit. Keep in mind that all spiritual things are known through intuition. However, to understand spiritual things is the work of the mind. Just as the soul has emotions, the spirit has spiritual feelings. The testimony within you is the method God uses most often to speak to you.

The Word of God says, *"The Spirit Himself bears witness with our spirit that we are children of God."* As a believer, you understand that when you die you will go to heaven. The testimony and intuition within you says that you are God's child.

Paul had a testimony

"23...except that the Holy Spirit testifies in every city, saying that chains and tribulations await me." Acts 20.23

The Apostle Paul never said, "The Holy Spirit spoke to me." He said, "The Holy Spirit testifies (I perceive, I feel in my spirit) prison is awaiting me."

Jesus had a testimony

"12 Immediately the Spirit drove Him into the wilderness." Mark 1.12

"8But immediately, when Jesus perceived in His spirit that they reasoned thus within themselves, He said to them, 'Why do you reason about these things in your hearts'?" Mark 2.8

The amplified Bible says, "And at once Jesus, becoming fully aware in His Spirit..." Jesus perceived, realized and was aware of, in His spirit, what they were harboring in their hearts.

Jesus is extremely pure and sensible in spirit. He understood what they were thinking. This type of perception doesn't come from an audible voice; it is a feeling of the heart. Jesus perceived it in His spirit.

I would like to share a few testimonies from my life on how God spoke to me through the inner witness.

Our testimony as a church

Miracle and Healing Crusade

From the moment I arrived at a healing and miracle crusade held in a school in Miami, Florida, I asked the Lord how He wanted to heal His people. I asked Him what method He wanted to use and how I should pray for the sick, that they may be healed. Did He want me to lay hands on them or did He want me to speak the Word? Immediately, I perceived in my spirit, or the witness within me led me to understand that I should lay hands on the sick. Again I asked the Lord, "How do you want me to pray for the sick?" The answer was the same, "Lay hands on people." However, when it was time to pray for the sick I did exactly the opposite. When I prayed for those who were sick, I only spoke the Word over them; nothing happened. At the end of the service, I called out to those who were in wheel chairs or walking with crutches. I laid hands on them. Suddenly, two people in wheel chairs stood up, three out of the four people using crutches laid them aside and started to walk without them. I returned home frustrated because only those people were healed. Immediately, God spoke to me saying, "Why did you disobey me? I told you to lay hands on the people, instead you spoke the word." This was the same instruction God gave Moses, "Speak to the rock." Moses did not obey God's instructions; instead, he struck the rock. Had I obeyed the witness in my spirit and laid hands on the people from the beginning of the service, God would have healed more people.

God Heals Eyes

On another occasion, while I was teaching a discipleship class in my church in Miami, I felt a sudden urge from the Holy Spirit that said, "Pray for the people who are suffering with eye problems." It was not a voice; it was a perception, an intuition. It was an understanding in my spirit to pray for those suffering with eye problems. Almost every person, who came forward for their healing, received it. Many were healed of cataracts, myopia, astigmatism, and more. Praise God when we obey the inner witness of the Holy Spirit!

Trip to Venezuela

A pastor friend of mine called and invited me to preach in Venezuela. During this time, their government was in turmoil. Strikes were going on everywhere and too many other situations to mention. When he said this to me, I felt the witness within my spirit; I perceived that I should not go. It was only a small impression in my spirit, which I chose not to listen. My wife had the same impression. She felt I should not go, but I purchased the ticket anyway and went. To my surprise, when I arrived in Venezuela, the government had declared a state of emergency. All public places were closed including churches. I wasted my time and money. I did not have the opportunity to preach. God wanted to spare me from the expenses of this trip, but I did not listen to the inner witness.

Sometimes, God reveals certain things He desires to do before each service. Other times, I feel like praising and worshipping. You need to learn to follow the leading of the inner witness, which is divinely given by the Holy Spirit. If you do this, you will experience victory in everything you do.

Another method God uses to speak to you is the voice of your conscience.

2. The Conscience

What is the conscience? It is another method used by God to speak to you. The conscience is the voice of your spirit.

It is the means, or the spiritual organ, given by God to help you discern between good and evil. The conscience is where God expresses His holiness. Through it, you perceive what is good and pleasing unto God. It is where sin is condemned and justice is approved. When we speak about your conscience as being the voice of your spirit, we are no longer talking about the inner witness, but of a voice within you, which rebukes you when you do something wrong and justifies you when you do something that is good and honest.

The moment that Adam committed the first sin he lost his intuition and communion with God. The only thing left in him was his conscience. As time passed, man's conscience became cauterized because of sin. He no longer hears the voice of his conscience because he is living in sin.

Faithfulness to our conscience is the first step to living in righteousness. A healthy conscience and the inner witness are inseparable.

To enjoy fellowship with God it is necessary for you to have a clean and purified conscience, washed by the blood of Jesus.

"14 ...how much more shall the blood of Christ, who through the eternal Spirit offered Himself without spot to God, cleanse your conscience from dead works to serve the living God?"
Hebrews 9.14

One offense in your conscience can block you from hearing the voice of God and your communion with Him. A conscience stained by an offense will be under constant accusation and will inevitably affect your relationship with God.

"20For if our heart condemns us, God is greater than our heart, and knows all things. 21Beloved, if our heart does not condemn us, we have confidence toward God." 1 John 3.20, 21

What things are certain believers doing to ignore the voice of their conscience?

Argue with it. They attempt to accumulate reasons to justify their actions and use excuses to alleviate their conscience. They refuse to accept what God is saying to them. They use expressions such as, "I don't tithe or give offerings because all pastors are thieves." They try to justify their actions to alleviate their conscience, thus disobeying the Word of God.

They ease their conscience by doing good works. Good works are performed in an effort to alleviate any guilty feelings sent by God that arise in their spirit, which inform them of their disobedience.

There are three types of conscience:

1. **A good conscience.** A good conscience does not stand accused before God. It is always ready and sensitive to hear God's voice.

2. **A weak conscience.** A weak conscience is easily contaminated, influenced and accused by the enemy. A person with a weak conscience constantly feels accused by the enemy.

3. **Cauterized conscience.** A cauterized **conscience** is at a level of indifference regarding sin. This is caused by the continuous act of sinning. An individual with a cauterized conscience will sin time and time again

without remorse. This type of individual eventually leaves the church and the Lord.

"[d] Now the Spirit expressly says that in latter times some will depart from the faith, giving heed to deceiving spirits and doctrines of demons, [2] speaking lies in hypocrisy, having their own conscience seared with a hot iron." 1 Timothy 4.1,2

If you are not careful to pay attention to the voice of your conscience when you are disciplined, and insist on living a sinful life, it could make you completely indifferent to His voice. Have you ever made a decision you regretted later on? Do you hear the voice of your conscience speaking and saying, "You shouldn't have done that!" Well, allow me to inform you, this was the voice of God speaking to your conscience letting you know that what you did was wrong. Your conscience will accuse you or defend you before God and your fellow brothers.

"[d5] ...who show the work of the law written in their hearts, their conscience also bearing witness, and between themselves their thoughts accusing or else excusing them." Romans 2.15

Paul had a good conscience

"[d] Then Paul, looking earnestly at the council, said, 'Men and brethren, I have lived in all good conscience before God until this day'." Acts 23.1

"[d2] For our boasting is this: the testimony of our conscience that we conducted ourselves in the world in simplicity and godly sincerity, not with fleshly wisdom but by the grace of God, and more abundantly toward you." 2 Corinthians 1.12

Paul had a good conscience. He knew when God was speaking to him and when he was doing what was pleasing and perfect before God.

My Testimony: It is customary for our church to have a healing and miracle crusade on the first Sunday of every month. One Sunday, we held a crusade outside of our church building. I was not satisfied with the results. I wanted more miracles, more healings and more salvations. As soon as I got home I started complaining to the Lord. I said, "I will never hold another healing and miracle crusade ever again. There were few salvations, healings or miracles. Lord, I will never have another service like this. I have to invest too much money. I fast, pray and I don't get the results I expect." When I was done complaining God spoke to my conscience. He said I was ungrateful and that I didn't appreciate the lives that were saved and healed. My conscience accused me. I felt awful before God. In other words, God was saying, "Your grumbling and complaining has reached my throne." I knew it was the Lord speaking to my conscience because I felt bad immediately. I asked the Lord to forgive me. I was genuinely sorry. Once I did this, every guilty feeling I was experiencing, disappeared. God spoke to my conscience and rebuked my actions. This was the voice of my spirit.

The conscience works according to the knowledge you have in the Word. Each time you receive revelation in a certain area of your life, the conscience is activated in that specific area. If you are faithful to your conscience, the voice of your spirit, you will walk in righteousness. If you have a guilt-free conscience, then you will have direct communication with God and the ability to hear His voice clearly.

How can you keep your conscience clean?

Every time you offend God, or sin against Him, you should repent and ask for His forgiveness immediately. As soon as you feel the tug in your conscience, repent and ask God to help you correct your mistake. This way, your conscience will remain clean and pure making it easy to hear God's voice.

A third method God uses to speak through us is the voice of the Holy Spirit.

3. The Voice of the Holy Spirit

You have learned that God speaks to you through the inner witness and your conscience, the voice of your spirit. Now let us study how God speaks to you using the voice of the Holy Spirit. Often, the Holy Spirit speaks to your life when He has something of supreme importance to communicate. It might have something to do with your calling; it might be a life or death situation; or something that will have a positive or negative effect on the lives of many people. It might also be something that is about to change the direction of a ministry or a vision. When God wants to speak to you, He makes sure that you are able to hear the voice of the Holy Spirit.

How does the voice of the Holy Spirit sound?

His voice is soft and tender. It carries great authority. At times, His voice sounds like someone is talking to you in a strong, audible voice. The Holy Spirit doesn't always speak to you directly, but when He does, you can be sure it is a specific time chosen by Him. Most of the time, He speaks to you through the inner witness. It comes from deep within you, from your spirit. His voice brings peace to your heart.

How can you tell the difference between the voice of the Holy Spirit and the voice of the enemy?

The Devil's Voice...

- Causes fear, anxiety and worry.
- Is always heard in the first person. This voice confuses you, making you believe that it is coming from your own mind. This is the way it deceives.
- Always contradicts God's Word
- Condemns
- Causes guilt
- Comes from outside the person

The Voice of God...

- Causes peace, quietness and tranquility
- Gives joy
- Is always in agreement with the Word of God
- Causes conviction, not condemnation
- Edifies, comforts and encourages
- Encourages unity between God and the individual
- The voice of the Holy Spirit comes from within

Biblical examples on how God spoke in the Old and New Testament.

- God spoke to Samuel.

"¹⁰Now the LORD came and stood and called as at other times, 'Samuel! Samuel!' And Samuel answered, 'Speak, for Your servant hears'." 1 Samuel 3.10

- God spoke to promote Paul and Barnabas.

"¹Now in the church that was at Antioch there were certain prophets and teachers: Barnabas, Simeon who was called Niger, Lucius of Cyrene, Manaen who had been brought up with Herod the tetrarch, and Saul. ²As they ministered to the Lord and fasted, the Holy Spirit said, 'Now separate to Me Barnabas and Saul for the work to which I have called them'. ³Then, having fasted and prayed, and laid hands on them, they sent them away." Acts 13.1-3

Personal Testimonies

A woman in Argentina. While preaching and teaching the Word of God in Argentina the Holy Spirit revealed to me that there was a woman in the audience who was contemplating suicide. When I finished my teaching, I began to pray for the people. I laid hands on them. When I approached one of the ladies in the prayer line, I immediately perceived in my spirit that she was the woman the Lord had spoken to me about. I prayed for her. During my prayer, the Lord spoke to my heart a specific word for her. He said He loved her very much. God said much more than that, but those few words touched her so deeply, that she broke down and cried. When the service was over, she approached me and said, "Pastor, I asked God to speak to me today. I was going through a desperate situation. I didn't know what to do. The only thing that came to mind was to say to God that if I didn't hear anything today I was going to walk out of this place and throw myself in front of a moving car. I was going to commit suicide." Praise God there was a word for that woman that stopped her from taking her own life! This miracle could only come from God.

The purchase of our church building. When I started as a pastor in my church, God blessed us with a place that had the capacity to fit 250 people. Each service was so well attended that a fourth service on Sunday had to be started immediately. The need for a bigger temple prompted me to begin praying and with the support of the congregation the Lord led us to a Jewish synagogue. When I saw it, I felt in my heart that this was the place God was showing us to purchase. The price for the synagogue was three million dollars. We didn't have anywhere near that amount. However, God put in my heart to gather the intercessors and to begin praying for our new temple.

On Friday, I called the intercessors and declared a prayer vigil; it was to be specifically for the temple. We started to pray at nine o'clock at night. The hours passed quickly; we were in fervent prayer and intercession. Suddenly, at two in the morning, the Holy Spirit powerfully descended upon us. We started shouting, jumping and laughing joyfully. This was what we were waiting for, a breakthrough in the spirit. I immediate walked up to the pulpit and declared what I heard the voice of the Holy Spirit say, "The victory is yours, and I have given you the temple."

I shared with the intercessors what the Lord had revealed to me. We rejoiced. Exactly one year after the Lord gave us the victory, we were moving to the new temple. God provided the money we needed to purchase it. God said it and it was done. The glory belongs to Him!

God provides for a woman in Argentina. At the end of a service held in Argentina, God spoke to me. He said, "Gather together a good offering and give it to the woman that will be waiting at the exit." As soon as I came close to the exit, I started to look around at the people gathered together. I noticed a woman who was praying and decided to approach her and ask her what she was praying for. She answered, "I am a single mother and I live alone with my children. I have no job or money to buy milk for my kids. I don't even have money to pay for the transportation I need to return home. I was just saying to the Lord that if He truly loved me, to provide an offering through the servant who preached the Word." I replied, "Sister, God spoke to me before walking out of the church. He said to give you this offering." This lady started to cry. God spoke and provided the money she needed to buy milk for her children and to pay her transportation. But the best of this story is the fact that in her prayer she asked God that the one to give her the offering be the pastor that had spoken that night. He should be the one to provide her with the money she needed. That pastor was me. Praise God, He is good!

Another method that God uses to speak to us is by use of His prophets.

4. The Prophets

The Prophetic ministry is still active today. It is given by the Lord Jesus Christ to edify the church. God raised up prophets in the Old and New Testament and continues to do so today. God is still talking to His people through the prophets.

• God spoke through the prophet Naaman.

"⁴⁰And Elisha sent a messenger to him, saying, 'Go and wash in the Jordan seven times, and your flesh shall be restored to you, and you shall be clean'." 2 Kings 5.10

- God spoke to Paul.

> "*10 And as we stayed many days, a certain prophet named Agabus came down from Judea. *11When he had come to us, he took Paul's belt, bound his own hands and feet, and said, 'Thus says the Holy Spirit, So shall the Jews at Jerusalem bind the man who owns this belt, and deliver him into the hands of the Gentiles'.*" Acts 21. 10-11*

What is a prophet?

A prophet is an extension of the ministry of Jesus and one of the five ministries of the Lord's government.

The prophet speaks in the name of the Lord. He will speak things regarding the past, present or future. He is one who speaks when urged and inspired by the Holy Spirit.

Personal testimony when land was purchased for the new temple.

I attended an apostolic congress on deliverance with Dr. Peter Wagner, in Colorado. There were approximately 25 people at this meeting. Those attending were ministers who believe and minister deliverance throughout the United States. Two days later, at the end of the meeting, we said our good-byes. But before leaving, my wife Ana, and I, approached Cindy Jacobs. She is an extraordinary prophetess of the Lord. She prophesized to us saying, "I see the Lord giving you a parcel of land, great in size, located in a very influential neighborhood in Kendall, in Miami. Surrounding this land are very expensive homes and a man-made lake. The Lord says He will give you this land." A short time later during one of our regular services, another prophet, Cathy Lechner, confirmed these words.

When she finished the prophecy, I made the comment that we would look for the land to buy it. There, we would build a bigger church. Upon my return to Miami, a real estate agent showed me a parcel of land with the same characteristics the prophets had mentioned. The land measured 37 acres. To make a long story short, this property had been in the market for many years. The owners of the land tried to sell it six times without success. We, as a church, were the seventh potential buyer (seven is God's number). We purchased the land at a price of 2.8 million dollars. This was exactly what the prophet had prophesied. At this moment, the design to build a structure that will house approximately 5,000 people is complete. God gave us the victory! He used a prophet to reveal what our property was going to look like. Praise God! He speaks to us today through His prophets.

There are many testimonies I could share with you of the times the Holy Spirit has spoken to me, but I prefer to continue with the other methods by which God still speaks to you.

5. Prophecy

Another method used by God to speak to you is through prophecy. Prophecy is a gift of the Holy Spirit and its purpose is to edify the body of Christ. God uses prophets and prophecy to speak to you.

What is prophecy?

Prophecy is the Hebrew word *"naba,"* meaning to flow forward, to bubble like a spring, to declare a truth that can only be revealed by divine revelation.

What is the biblical definition of prophecy?

Prophecy is a gift of the Holy Spirit given to the believer to speak a word inspired by God. Its purpose is to exhort, comfort and edify the body of Christ.

What is the difference between the gift of prophecy and the office of the prophet?

The office of the prophet is one of the five ministerial gifts that make up the government of the church. The ministry of the prophet is not a gift of the Holy Spirit, but an extension of Christ as a prophet. Prophecy is a gift given by the Holy Spirit. Jesus is the full manifestation of the five offices or ministerial gifts in a ministry.

"11 And He Himself gave some to be apostles, some prophets, some evangelists, and some pastors and teachers." Ephesians 4.11

It is important to remember that prophecy is a gift of the Holy Spirit given to an individual. The prophet is a ministerial gift, an office given to the body.

What is the purpose of prophecy in the New Testament?

"3 But he who prophesies speaks edification and exhortation and comfort to men. 4 He who speaks in a tongue edifies himself, but he who prophesies edifies the church." 1 Corinthians 14.3, 4

- **To edify.** The word "edify" literally means to lift up. It goes beyond speaking in other tongues, which only edifies you. The prophetic word raises up the spirit, the state of mind and the attitude. Its purpose is to strengthen you when you are discouraged and burdened.

- **To encourage.** In the Greek language, the word "encourage" means a call to approach, come close, to comfort and to assure. When you receive the prophetic word, you are encouraged to keep going and to get closer to God.

- **To comfort.** The word "comfort" means to receive relief in the midst of tribulation or difficulty. The prophetic word brings us assurance and comfort during difficult times. God still speaks to us using the prophetic word. The gift of prophecy is alive today; to activate it, the only thing we have to do is believe it, and act upon it.

In addition to prophesy, God speaks to us through the written Word.

6. The Word of God or Scripture

"²⁰My son, keep your father's command, and do not forsake the law of your mother. ²¹Bind them continually upon your heart; tie them around your neck. ²²When you roam, they will lead you; when you sleep, they will keep you; and when you awake, they will speak with you." Proverbs 6.20-22

God often speaks through the written Word. Sometimes, a verse will surface in your heart and it will be exactly the answer you were looking for. Other times, people will approach you and give you a specific word from scripture, which will be God's exact answer to your need.

Sometimes, you will go to church facing a difficult situation. Suddenly, the pastor will begin to preach or recite verses from Scripture that speak directly to your problem. This is God speaking to you.

God is still talking to us. One method He uses is through the Bible. During our personal or corporate prayer time, He will bring to mind Biblical passages that will speak directly to our spirit. It is crucial to be continually filled with His Word, to confess it, believe it and act upon it. This is how God will speak directly into our heart; through His Word.

Another method God often uses to speak to us is through dreams.

7. Dreams

In the past, God used dreams to speak to His people. He is still using them. God has spoken important things concerning His kingdom. My wife is a perfect example of how God speaks to His people through dreams. Almost every time my wife says she had a dream, it's because God has spoken to her.

What are dreams?

The Webster dictionary defines "dreams" as the succession of images or ideas present in the mind while sleeping.

Dreams are formed in your subconscious. They depend on your background, experience and circumstances. This is how images and symbols are formed; they are unique to you. Dreams are strictly organized in the natural mind. They can also be images given by God and the Holy Spirit; these are received in your mind. They are not always easy to understand, but through your dreams God speaks to you. For example, God spoke to Joseph in a dream.

"⁶Now Joseph had a dream, and he told it to his brothers; and they hated him even more." Genesis 37.5

In addition to dreams, God also speaks to us through visions.

8. Visions

The Webster dictionary defines "vision" as the act or ability to see abstract or invisible objects. There are other Greek and Hebrew words that can also be used to describe what the word "vision" means. One of those words is revelation. When God allows you to see in the spiritual realm, it's because you are receiving a revelation from God. This is similar to watching television images in full color.

Dreams and visions are evidence that the Holy Spirit is active. It is also a sign of the outpouring of the Holy Spirit in the last days.

"¹⁶But this is what was spoken by the prophet Joel: ¹⁷'And it shall come to pass in the last days, says God, that I will pour out of My Spirit on all flesh; your sons and your daughters shall prophesy, your young men shall see visions, your old men shall dream dreams'." Acts 2.16, 17

There are three types of visions:

- **Spiritual vision.** This type of vision is when you are able to see in the spiritual realm, as Paul did, when he was traveling to Damascus. Paul said that when the vision came, his eyes were blinded. He was unable to see with his physical eyes, yet he was able to see in the spirit. God also spoke to Ananias through a vision telling him to go and pray for Paul.

[10]Now there was a certain disciple at Damascus named Ananias; and to him the Lord said in a vision, 'Ananias'. And he said, 'Here I am, Lord'." Acts 9.10

- **Trance.** During this vision the physical senses are suspended. This is the second most important type of vision you might experience. You are not aware of your surroundings or the physical world. It's not that you are unconscious, on the contrary, you are intensely aware of spiritual things; more than physical things.

  Example: When Paul went to Jerusalem he said to the people, *"Now it happened, when I returned to Jerusalem and was praying in the temple, that I was in a **trance** [18] and saw Him saying to me, make haste and get out of Jerusalem quickly, for they will not receive your testimony concerning Me." Acts 22.17, 18*

- **The conscientious vision.** During this vision, all the senses are in operation; your eyes are open. This is the most important type of vision you might experience. You are conscious of everything around you. You are also able to see into the spiritual realm. The Old Testament Prophets were called seers; they often had this type of vision.

  [9]Formerly in Israel, when a man went to inquire of God, he spoke thus: "Come, let us go to the seer"; for he who is now called a prophet was formerly called a seer." 1 Samuel 9.9

What are the sources of inspiration for dreams and visions?

It is important to remember that dreams and visions come from three different sources:

- Dreams and visions inspired by the Holy Spirit.
- Dreams and visions created by your soul.
- Dreams and visions created by the enemy.

Dreams and spiritual visions, inspired by the Holy Spirit and made known by the natural mind, deliver a specific message. It could be a revelation or something else. I believe you should ask God, through prayer, to help you interpret the dreams and visions you believe are from God.

God spoke to Peter through a vision.

[9]The next day, as they went on their journey and drew near the city, Peter went up on the housetop to pray, about the sixth hour. [10]Then he became very hungry and wanted to eat; but while they made ready, he fell into a trance [11]and saw heaven opened and an object like a great sheet bound at the four corners, descending to him and let down to the earth. [12]In it were all kinds of four-footed animals of the earth, wild beasts, creeping things, and birds of the air. [13]And a voice came to him, 'Rise, Peter; kill and eat'. [14]But Peter said, 'Not so, Lord! For I have never eaten anything common or unclean'. [15]And a voice spoke to him again the second time, 'What God has cleansed you must not call common'. [16]This was done three times. And the object was taken up into heaven again."
Acts 10.9-16

Once more, the Word confirms that God speaks to you through dreams and visions. God lives and continues to speak to His people. It is very important for you to understand which method He is using to speak to you.

At times, another way God speaks to us is through angelic visitation.

9. Angels

Throughout the Old Testament it was common for God to speak to His people through angels. The Word of God teaches that they are ministering spirits sent to serve the saints. This is another method used by God to speak to you.

"14Are they not all ministering spirits sent forth to minister for those who will inherit salvation?" Hebrews 1.14

Angels are not commonly used by God to send messages. But, in special circumstances, you may have seen and heard that God has sent His angels to deliver a specific message to His people. One example is when God sent His angel to tell Mary about the birth of Jesus.

"28And having come in, the angel said to her, "Rejoice, highly favored one, the Lord is with you; blessed are you among women!" Luke 1.28

Another method God uses to speak to us is through an inner sense of peace.

10. Inner Peace

God often speaks to me through the testimony of inner peace. Once I make a decision and have no peace about it in my heart, I receive it as a sign from God letting me know that the decision I made was not the right one. When there is an uneasiness, preoccupation or lack of peace in my spirit, it is like an alarm clock going off inside of me as evidence that there is no inner peace. If I don't feel that inner peace, I prefer not to do what I had planned on doing.

What is peace?

The word "peace" comes from the Hebrew root word *"shalam"* and this word comes from the root word *"shalom,"* meaning to be sure, complete, secure, at ease and strengthened. Knowing the definition of this word helps you to understand that when you have that kind of restful feeling, quietness and assurance in your spirit concerning something, it usually means God is talking to you. We should strive to have that inner peace.

"¹⁴Pursue peace with all people, and holiness, without which no one will see the Lord." Hebrews 12.14

"¹Let him turn away from evil and do good; Let him seek peace and pursue it." 1 Peter 3.11

God is trying to say that you should seek that inner peace wholeheartedly. You should do everything within your power to have peace with God, others and yourselves. Wanting to feel that inner peace should not be a simple desire, but an intense search. It will help you make the right decisions; such decisions glorify God and bring victory into your life.

There are two things the peace of God will do in your life:

• **Keeps your heart and mind.**

"⁷...and the peace of God, which surpasses all understanding, will guard your hearts and minds through Christ Jesus." Philippians 4.7

- **Governs your hearts.**

"15...and let the peace of God rule in your hearts, to which also you were called in one body; and be thankful."
Colossians 3.15

When God's peace governs your mind and heart, you will be able to make wise decisions that will glorify God.

Now that you understand the methods God uses to speak to His people, it is easy to see why God is a personal God and that He speaks to you in different ways using different methods.

We can end this chapter with the understanding that God speaks to us. He uses methods such as feelings, hearing and sight to communicate. He also uses different methods to speak because He is a sovereign God. He uses the best method to communicate His plans and His perfect will. Ask yourself the following question, "What method does God use to speak to me?" Could it be the inner witness; the conscience; the voice of the Holy Spirit; prophecy or the prophets? Could it be through dreams or visions? Perhaps through angels, or the written Word of God? You need to become familiar with the method God is using to speak to you. You must learn to hear the voice of God!

How can you sharpen your spiritual ears to hear the voice of God?

Walk in the Spirit. Your spiritual "antennas" should always be ready to hear what He has to say. You should be constantly tuned in. The only way this is accomplished is through steadfast prayer in the spirit.

You should act by faith. Sometimes it is difficult to understand what God is saying. Don't wait to feel something or to see with your natural eyes before obeying. Believe, by faith, and do what God is asking you to do.

"But without faith it is impossible to please Him, for he who comes to God must believe that He is, and that He is a rewarder of those who diligently seek Him." Hebrews 11.6

God wants to share His plans, purpose and will. For this to happen, you must obey Him, walk in the Spirit and act by faith. Don't reason what He is asking you to do, just do it by faith.

CHAPTER III

How to Walk in the Supernatural

n this chapter you will learn how to walk in the supernatural. You will also understand why many believers can't move in the realm of the supernatural. When we talk about the supernatural, we are referring to everything that has to do with the prophetic ministry.

What does prophetic mean?

The prophetic expresses the heart and mind of God in a supernatural dimension. The prophetic is not standing up in front of a congregation and saying, "The Lord says," then declaring the prophetic word to someone in specific. This is only half of it; there is much more to it than that. To move in the prophetic means to express and demonstrate the supernatural nature of God and bring it into a physical and tangible dimension. The Apostle Paul went to Corinth in the prophetic; he demonstrated the supernatural nature of the mind and heart of God.

"⁴And my speech and my preaching were not with persuasive words of human wisdom, but in demonstration of the Spirit and of power, ⁵that your faith should not be in the wisdom of men but in the power of God." 1 Corinthians 2.4, 5

In these verses, the Apostle explains once more, the reason why the Word and the preaching were not persuasive words spoken through human wisdom, but rather they were a demonstration of the Holy Spirit and power.

"⁶That your faith should not be in the wisdom of men but in the power of God." 1 Corinthians 2.5

What does the prophetic or supernatural involve?

- Prophecy
- Healing
- Casting out demons
- Hearing the voice of God
- To hear, feel and see from God
- Moving in the gifts of the Holy Spirit
- Preaching the gospel
- Miracles
- Signs
- Wonders

Unfortunately, few ministers and believers move in the supernatural. Because of their ignorance concerning the prophetic, churches are founded on human wisdom. They tell others about healing, but no one receives their healing; they speak of prophecy, yet, they silence the men and women of God that rise up and prophesy in the church. They are unwilling to adopt the supernatural move in their churches. This stops the prophetic from revealing itself, which is the supernatural nature of God. They need the supernatural manifestations of the Holy Spirit to persuade the minds and emotions of the congregation that they may be established on the power of God. They choose reason, intellectual thinking and man-made programs over the supernatural.

Why are believers not moving in the supernatural?

Let us take a look at the obstacles that believers face today, which block them from moving in the supernatural.

1. Lack of knowledge

"Now concerning spiritual gifts, brethren, I do not want you to be ignorant." 1 Corinthians 12.1

The word "ignorant" means lacking knowledge. This doesn't mean total lack of knowledge, but that the knowledge available can't be applied to daily living. Many crave and desire to walk into the supernatural dimension, but have no idea how to do it. Lack of knowledge destroys God's people.

2. Doubt and unbelief

"¹⁸And to whom did He swear that they would not enter His rest, but to those who did not obey? ¹⁹So we see that they could not enter in because of unbelief." Hebrews 3.18, 19

The Word of God teaches that signs and wonders follow those who believe. What signs and wonders? Healing the sick, casting out demons, prophesizing, speaking in other tongues and performing creative miracles. It is important to emphasize that, "These signs will follow those who believe." They will not follow the unbelievers. If you think that healing miracles can not happen today, if you don't believe in miracles at all, don't worry, nothing is ever going to happen to you or through you.

There is great hunger throughout the world to understand the supernatural. Because of this, many seek after witches, palm readers, Santeros and psychics for solutions to their problems; they are searching for something or someone who can tell them about their personal life. Why are believers seeking for the supernatural in occultism instead of the church?

Because the church doesn't believe in the supernatural and if it doesn't believe, it can't demonstrate the supernatural nature of God.

What should you do?

You must believe God wants and desires to express the supernatural through His church. He wants to demonstrate prophecy, healing miracles, signs and wonders, and casting out demons. God wants to show these things, but He is only able to do it through you and me.

3. **Fear of making mistakes**

"⁶Therefore I remind you to stir up the gift of God which is in you through the laying on of my hands. ⁷For God has not given us a spirit of fear, but of power and of love and of a sound mind." 2 Timothy 1.6, 7

A certain level of faith is needed to move in the supernatural. Many people are afraid of making mistakes. They worry too much about their image and what people think of them. For this reason, they don't dare to move in the supernatural.

One way the enemy binds you is by making you think that you have to do everything right; he wants to deceive you into thinking that you are not allowed to make mistakes. This is precisely the reason why you might be afraid to prophesy, pray for the sick and cast out demons. You think you have to do everything perfect. Allow me to take this opportunity to inform you that the only way to move in the supernatural is by learning through your mistakes. At some point, you will be wrong; at this time, you must learn to walk in faith. Every time God asks you to do something and you feel afraid to do it, rebuke the spirit of fear and begin to act in faith.

4. Feeling unworthy

It is easy to believe that God can use other people, but not you. You see yourself as an unworthy sinner. Because of this, you believe that God is unable to use you.

The reason God uses you is not because of your great abilities, titles or diplomas. He doesn't use you because you have the "right" family background or because you're intelligent or charismatic. He uses you because He wants to. None of the things previously mentioned are valid before God. It is only because of His grace and favor that He uses you. He is the one who makes you worthy.

God wants to use you; dare to believe Him! He is raising up an army of men and women who dare to walk in the power of the Holy Spirit and the supernatural. This army must believe without fear of making mistakes. If Christ makes you worthy, then you must be worthy. Dare to walk in the supernatural!

5. The influence of the spirit of Greece

The spirit of Greece is the number one enemy of the supernatural. Its influence on the church of Christ has paralyzed the prophetic and all things concerning the supernatural. Let us study the spirit of Greece in depth.

"²⁰Then he said, 'Do you know why I have come to you? And now I must return to fight with the prince of Persia; and when I have gone forth, indeed the prince of Greece will come. ²¹But I will tell you what is noted in the Scripture of Truth. No one upholds me against these, except Michael your prince'." Daniel 10.20, 21

"¹²Return to the stronghold, you prisoners of hope. Even today I declare that I will restore double to you. ¹³For I have bent Judah, My bow, fitted the bow with Ephraim, and raised up your sons, O Zion, against your sons, O Greece, and made you like the sword of a mighty man." Zechariah 9.12, 13

The spirit of Greece

After the death of the apostles in the year 100 AC, the spirit of Greece began to infiltrate the church. The Greek world, in which the apostles ministered, was full of such philosophies. The Greeks loved wisdom. They desired knowledge to such extremes, that they developed an idolatrous mind. In other words, they adored knowledge. The word philosophy comes from Greece and it means the love of knowledge.

Greek society produced Aristotle, Plato and many more philosophers. They would engage in great debates or arguments trying to defend their points of view. They loved to debate and to reason. The church was birthed in this kind of a world. It was only through God's grace and the apostolic anointing that the church received the ability to defeat this mentality.

The spirit of Greece operates like a rigid structure based on reasoning and human qualities, whose only objective is to become "superman" or "super gods"!

This spirit manifests itself in the form of a thought, thus limiting the believer to enter the Kingdom of God and its supernatural dimensions. During the days of the apostles, the world was politically controlled by the Romans, but culturally influenced by the Greek. They were the greatest strongholds faced by the church. The spirits of intellectualism and rationalism deceived many into believing that Jesus had not risen from the dead. The universities that existed during that time were full of these spirits. The spirits of intellectualism, rationalism, pride, spirits that provoke debate and idolatrous minds, also govern many educational systems today. The first apostles had to confront these spirits and we are not exempt from that. As Christians in today's society, we face the same opposition. We must learn to deal with it.

The goddesses Athena, Sophia and Diana form the basic structure that binds this stronghold.

Athena: the Greek goddess who hated anything that had to do with the apostolic, the prophetic and the supernatural.

Sophia: the goddess of wisdom and love of knowledge, among other things.

Diana: the goddess of religion or as she is commonly known, the goddess of heaven.

Let us look at Scripture to see what it has to say:

"⁵...casting down arguments and every high thing that exalts itself against the knowledge of God, bringing every thought into captivity to the obedience of Christ." 2 Corinthians 10.5

One translations says, *"[Inasmuch as we] refute arguments and theories and reasonings and every proud and lofty thing that sets itself up against the [true] knowledge of God; and we lead every thought and purpose away captive into the obedience of Christ (the Messiah, the Anointed One)."*

Greek philosophers known as the "Sophists" specialized in rhetoric, dialectic and argumentation. They were teachers, philosophers and professionals who loved to elaborate complicated arguments. Sophism is a deception from the devil. This philosophy gained popularity among the Greek because while the Jews were waiting for signs, they searched for wisdom.

"22For Jews request a sign, and Greeks seek after wisdom."
1 Corinthians 1.22

The Greek mentality flooded the western world, the United States of America and Europe with their philosophy. The purpose of this spirit was to take over and govern the entire world.

What are some of the characteristics of the Greek culture or the spirit of Greece?

- **Humanism.** Heraclitus introduced this philosophy when he replaced God with man. He removed God from His throne and placed man on it, as if man were a god. The New Age movement is the perfect example of this philosophy. It teaches that man is God, that he is self-sufficient and that he does not need a supreme being to exist.

- **Intellectualism.** This philosophy teaches that academic degrees, titles, recognition and wealth are more important that anything else, including God.

The ability to rationalize, according to the Greek mentality, is what rules the universe. Its goal is to develop man's intellectual abilities until he believes he has become a god in his own right. Intellectualism continues to control the mentality of eastern society, countries of the former Soviet Union, Europe and other countries.

What are the components of intellectualism?

* **Intellectualism denies everything that can't be explained.** It rejects and abolishes the concept of living by faith because it can't be scientifically explained. This is one of the reasons the church has lost its power, because it is easier to believe in the things that can be seen with the natural eye, than to believe in what can't be seen. The Word of God commands you to live by faith and not by sight.

"Behold the proud, his soul is not upright in him; but the just shall live by his faith." Habakkuk 2.4

"For we walk by faith, not by sight." 2 Corinthians 5.7

* **It denies the existence of demons, thus becoming a stumbling block for a believer's deliverance.** Unfortunately, the enemy holds in bondage many believers because their pastors refuse to believe in deliverance or demons. One great lie of the enemy, among many, is the one that says demons don't exist. The church has believed this lie. Let us see through the following verse how Jesus dealt with demons.

"22And behold, a woman of Canaan came from that region and cried out to Him, saying, "Have mercy on me, O Lord, Son of David! My daughter is severely demon-possessed."

HOW TO HEAR THE VOICE OF GOD

[23]But He answered her not a word. And His disciples came and urged Him, saying, "Send her away, for she cries out after us." [24]But He answered and said, "I was not sent except to the lost sheep of the house of Israel." [25]Then she came and worshiped Him, saying, "Lord, help me!" [26]But He answered and said, "It is not good to take the children's bread and throw it to the little dogs." [27]And she said, "Yes, Lord, yet even the little dogs eat the crumbs which fall from their masters' table." [28]Then Jesus answered and said to her, "O woman, great is your faith! Let it be to you as you desire." And her daughter was healed from that very hour."
Matthew 15.22-28

- **It resists the supernatural.** This is the most important characteristic I want you to understand. One reason why many ministers and believers can't walk in the supernatural is because the influence of the spirit of Greece is so strong.

- **It denies divine healing.** The people of the Bible (the Jews) were trained by God to see extraordinary and supernatural things. Our God is a supernatural and powerful God who does miracles, heals, and shows us signs and wonders. He casts demons out and prophesizes. His essence is supernatural. We, as His people, must learn to move in the same dimension as He does. Unfortunately, the influence of the spirit of Greece is so powerful that it has created strongholds in our minds, blocking us from receiving salvation, healing and deliverance. Instead, we have chosen to reason things out and whatever we don't understand, we simply choose not to believe. We must renounce the spirit of Greece if we truly desire to see the supernatural.

- **It rejects the gifts of the Holy Spirit.** Today, it is uncommon to see believers flow in the gifts of the Holy Spirit. Many might talk about it, but few believe it themselves.

- **It humanizes the Word of God.** The spirit of Greece declares that the Word of God is the same as the word of any ordinary man. The Hebrew mentality declares that God is a supernatural God and not a man that He should be explained. This was the mentality Jesus established when He demonstrated the supernatural in God.

How can we be delivered from the spirit of Greece?

- Renouncing to all strongholds coming from this spirit.

- Declaring warfare against this spirit with the power of God.

"[12] Return to the stronghold, you prisoners of hope. even today I declare that I will restore double to you. [13] For I have bent Judah, My bow, fitted the bow with Ephraim, and raised up your sons, O Zion, against your sons, o Greece, and made you like the sword of a mighty man." Zechariah 9.12-13

Demonstrating how to rebuke demons and operating in the gifts of the Holy Spirit is the antidote against the spirit of Greece, which denies the supernatural. You know you have a wonderful and powerful God who still does wonderful deeds.

How to activate a believer in the prophetic or the supernatural.

What is activation?

Activation is to encourage the believer to receive divine grace and to act upon the Word of God.

This principle is used to activate the gifts. One mortal being has the ability to activate another mortal being.

For example: an evangelist guides a sinner in the prayer of repentance. At that moment, the gift of eternal life is activated in the person receiving Jesus as Lord. This gift comes from God and is activated by the evangelist.

"⁸For by grace you have been saved through faith, and that not of yourselves; it is the gift of God." Ephesians 2.8

If you believe that once you guide a person through the sinner's prayer, he/she is activated in the supernatural or in any other gift, then you can believe anything.

Does activation really work?

When you received the Lord, someone had to guide you through the sinner's prayer. You believed this confession was genuine and that the gift of eternal life was received at that moment. It's the same way for the supernatural. You believe, by faith, in the gifts of the Holy Spirit, miracles, prophecies and more. When the revelation comes by faith, the gift is received and you are activated.

What should you do when someone expresses his or her desire to receive the gift of tongues?

The first thing you should do is to lay hands on the person and pray for him to receive the gift of tongues. As the revelation of this gift comes upon him, his understanding will be enlightened. The person believes that this revelation and gift is real and receives the gift of tongues by faith. You can activate anybody in the supernatural with the gifts of the Holy Spirit, miracles, prophecies, healing, signs, wonders and more.

What are the four ingredients needed to activate a believer in the supernatural or in the prophetic?

1. **Hear the Word of God.** Faith needed to activate a believer in the supernatural only comes when the Word of God is heard first. If you desire to walk in any area of the supernatural, you will not be effective unless you hear the Word for that specific area.

    "[d7] So then faith comes by hearing, and hearing by the Word of God." Romans 10.17

2. **Confess with your mouth.** Confession is the bridge that connects and activates the spiritual and the physical worlds. This declaration reveals the extreme importance of making the confession of faith in Jesus a public one. This public confession loosens the power of God to do what the Word says it can do. If you desire to operate in the supernatural, you must begin to confess what God says regarding prophecy, miracles and healing.

    "[8] But what does it say? 'The word is near you, in your mouth and in your heart' (that is, the word of faith which we preach): [9] that if you confess with your mouth the Lord Jesus and believe in your heart that God has raised Him from the dead, you will be saved. [10] For with the heart one believes unto righteousness,

and with the mouth confession is made unto salvation."
Romans 10. 8-10

3. **Believe in your heart.** Believing implies to act on faith according to what you hear, believe and confess. For this reason, before you receive salvation, the following ingredients must be present first: believe wholeheartedly, in other words, make the commitment and embrace it. Make this covenant a part of what you are.

4. **Make a corresponding action.** The following Scripture demonstrates how the woman with the issue of blood made a corresponding action to receive her healing.

"27When she heard about Jesus, she came behind Him in the crowd and touched His garment." Mark 5.27

This woman approached Jesus from behind and touched His robe with conviction. She knew that if she were successful, she would receive what she needed. She believed what she heard, acted upon that belief, and received what she asked for.

The principles mentioned above are needed to activate a person to receive the gift of eternal life. These same principles are also needed to activate a person to receive any gift of the Holy Spirit or to activate him in the supernatural.

The ability to walk in the supernatural may be received by a mortal man or woman. It is activated when the Word is heard, confessed with the mouth, believed in the heart and followed with a corresponding action based upon that Word.

CHAPTER IV

Gifts of the Holy Spirit

$\mathcal{T}$he most frequently asked question concerning the Holy Spirit is, "Do all believers have a gift?" The answer is yes. Every believer has been given a specific gift to bless the body of Christ. In this chapter you will learn why the gifts of the Holy Spirit are given to believers.

What is the purpose for the gifts of the Holy Spirit?

1. **To edify and build up the church.** God has given you gifts to help you grow and be edified as a church.

   "⁷But the manifestation of the Spirit is given to each one for the profit of all." 1 Corinthians 12.7

2. **To glorify Jesus.** The gifts of the Holy Spirit are given to the believer to glorify Jesus in everything, not to exalt or glorify man or a specific ministry.

   "¹¹If anyone speaks, let him speak as the oracles of God. If anyone ministers, let him do it as with the ability which God supplies, that in all things God may be glorified through Jesus Christ, to whom belong the glory and the dominion forever and ever. Amen." 1 Peter 4.11

3. **To evangelize effectively.** The Word of God teaches that the gospel is not empty words, but it is the power of God. The society in which we live in is only interested in witnessing signs and wonders. You need to give them a visible demonstration of the

power of God. I believe God has given you gifts to equip the church and to reach the lost effectively.

"15And He said to them, "Go into all the world and preach the gospel to every creature. 16He who believes and is baptized will be saved; but he who does not believe will be condemned. 17And these signs will follow those who believe: In My name they will cast out demons; they will speak with new tongues; 18they will take up serpents; and if they drink anything deadly, it will by no means hurt them; they will lay hands on the sick, and they will recover." Mark 16.15-18

4. **To deliver people from bondage.** The gifts of the Holy Spirit are given to the believer for the deliverance of His people from bondage, oppressions and generational curses. A word of knowledge given by the Holy Spirit is sufficient to reveal the yoke of the enemy against a person. Once this yoke is brought to light, the person is delivered by the power of God!

Can you operate in the gifts of the Holy Spirit whenever you want to?

"11But one and the same Spirit works all these things, distributing to each one individually as He wills." 1 Corinthians 12.11

Ancient Pentecostal believers misused this verse. They claimed to be unable to operate in the gifts of the Spirit unless the Holy Spirit **"wanted them to"**. They believed that if they didn't feel, see or hear anything, then it was impossible to operate in the gifts. What they were trying to say was that you could only prophesy if the Holy Spirit wanted you to do it. This is not what the Scripture says.

The key phrase **"*distributing as He wills*"** needs to be analyzed carefully. One thing is to operate in the gifts of the Holy Spirit when you want to and another to operate in the gifts you want. This section of verse 11 shows that you don't choose the gift that you want. God gives you the gift that He wants to give you. The Holy Spirit distributes His gifts according to His sovereign will.

"¹⁸But now God has set the members, each one of them, in the body just as He pleased." 1 Corinthians 12.18

This verse clearly states that the Holy Spirit chooses and distributes His gifts according to His will. You can't say, "I want to be an apostle, I want the gift of miracles, or I want the gift of healing." The Holy Spirit is the only one who distributes His gifts according to His will. However, for these gifts to operate it is necessary that you surrender your will to God and to have faith.

You don't have to wait until you feel, hear or see something to move in the gifts of the Spirit. You can prophesy by faith. Once you receive a gift, if you really have it, then you must use it. Your ability to use this gift depends on three things:

- **Faith.** If you believe you have the gift, then you must act accordingly whenever the opportunity arises.
- **Flowing with the gift.** You must allow the gift to manifest through you.
- **Believe.** You must act on what you believe.

Operating in the gifts doesn't depend on the Spirit when you act in faith and surrender to the leading of the Holy Spirit. When you believe wholeheartedly, the gift is manifested. The Word of God that says, *"...as the Spirit wills"* is referring to the distribution of the gifts not on how to operate in them.

Let us take a look at a few examples:

Do you believe you can speak in tongues when you want to?

"14For if I pray in a tongue, my spirit prays, but my understanding is unfruitful. 15What is the conclusion then? I will pray with the spirit, and I will also pray with the understanding. I will sing with the spirit, and I will also sing with the understanding."
1 Corinthians 14.14-15

In a modern translation of a Spanish Bible this verse reads as follows: "Paul says, *'I, voluntarily (of my own accord) will pray in other tongues and I will pray with the understanding. I, (voluntarily) will sing in the spirit or in tongues and I will also sing in my own understanding'."*

Paul didn't say, "When I feel something, then I will praise and sing in tongues." He said, "I do it when I want to." **The gifts are given by the Holy Spirit, but are activated only by your faith.**

You can operate in the gifts of the Spirit including prophecy, miracles and healing the same way you operate in the gift of tongues, when you want to. All the gifts are activated by faith. God always wants to speak, heal and deliver, and when He finds a willing vessel, He will use it.

Jesus is the head of the church. He appoints the five-fold ministry. The Holy Spirit distributes the five gifts or ministerial offices, and the believer activates them by faith, under the total direction of the Heavenly Father.

What should be your attitude towards the Gifts of the Holy Spirit?

Some believers have a very passive and indifferent attitude towards the gifts, but the Word of God teaches what your attitude should be concerning them.

1. **Don't ignore anything that has to do with the gifts.** The word "ignorant" in Greek is *"agnoeo,"* meaning to not recognize, know, or be familiarized with. It means to lack information or the functional knowledge that allows you to experiment. What the apostle Paul was saying in Corinthians is: "I want you to know, to be familiarized with, to be informed, to have revealed knowledge of the gifts in order for you to be able to flow in them. This way you will be able to experience what it means to operate in the gifts.

   "ᵈNow concerning spiritual gifts, brethren, I do not want you to be ignorant." 1 Corinthians 12.1

   Understanding the gifts of the Holy Spirit is the starting point for the manifestation of the gifts by faith.

2. **Desire the best gifts.** The word desire in Greek is *"zeloo,"* meaning to have a great desire to see something happen. It is an instinct that motivates you to see beyond your ability to imagine. This passion helps you to forget your self-image. You will no longer care what others think of you. This passion is so strong, it makes you yearn, desire and want to see the manifestation of the gifts in your life.

   "³¹But earnestly desire the best gifts. And yet I show you a more excellent way." 1 Corinthians 12.31

Desire is the key to receiving what you want from God.

"24Therefore I say to you, whatever things you ask when you pray, believe that you receive them, and you will have them." Mark 11.24

Spiritual gifts are the only divine attribute or spiritual blessing that the apostle Paul tells the people in Corinth to wish for.

3. **Stir up the gifts within you.** The word *"anazopureo"* means to light up again, to keep the flame alive. The apostle Paul is telling Timothy to light up or stir the fire within him again. If Paul said this, then this must mean that the gift Timothy received the day he was ordained and which was imparted by the presbytery had died out. This teaches you that your gift, given by God, must be kept alive for Him.

"6Therefore I remind you to stir up the gift of God which is in you through the laying on of my hands." 2 Timothy 1.6

Reviving the gift that is in you is based on your will and not on God's will. Also, an apostle of God can activate the gifts in you.

How can you revive the gift inside of you?

God gives you a gift with the desire to use you through it. Don't be afraid to make mistakes when you use it. Activate your gift through faith and God's grace. Begin practicing your gift today; remember the gift is developed only when you use it. Therefore, begin asking God in prayer to give you a thought or an impression concerning an individual and begin to use your gift now!

4. **The gifts are developed through practice and use.** You can't develop your spiritual gifts or flow in God's grace unless you practice using your gift continually. Many believers have the gift of prophecy and the gift of miracles, but they are not using them, and this keeps the gift from developing. Discernment is perfected only through practice and not simply through teaching and preaching.

> *"[14]But solid food belongs to those who are of full age, that is, those who by reason of use have their senses exercised to discern both good and evil." Hebrews 5.14*

5. **The gifts should not be neglected.** You should never neglect the gift God gives you. You should not abuse it or use it unwisely. God will hold you accountable for it. I have met many believers with the gift of miracles, healing, prophecy, discernment of spirit and others. Unfortunately, because of their neglect of their gifts, they became inactive.

> *"[14]Do not neglect the gift that is in you, which was given to you by prophecy with the laying on of the hands of the eldership." 1 Timothy 4.14*

God gives you gifts for you to use, to edify the church and to glorify Jesus. Because it is He who gives them, you should not remain ignorant concerning the gifts. You should deeply desire to have the gifts and to keep them active because as you use them, they will increase in your life.

Let us take a look at what the Word of God has to say:

"¹⁰As each one has received a gift, minister it to one another, as good stewards of the manifold grace of God." 1Peter 4.10

You can categorize the gifts of the Holy Spirit in three different categories. God does something different with each one.

GIFTS OF POWER	INSPIRATIONAL GIFTS	GIFTS OF REVELATION
• Gift of Faith	• Prophecy	• Word of Science or Knowledge
• Gift of Healing	• Different kinds of Tongues	• Word of Wisdom
• Gift of Miracles	• Interpretation of Tongues	• Discernment of Spirits

Gifts of Power

*G*od is doing something through these gifts: *"⁹...to another faith by the same Spirit, to another gifts of healings by the same Spirit, 10to another the working of miracles, to another prophecy, to another discerning of spirits, to another different kinds of tongues, to another the interpretation of tongues." 1 Corinthians 12.9-10*

What is the gift of faith?

1. **The Gift of Faith.** It is the supernatural manifestation of the Holy Spirit given to a believer, which enables him to believe as God believes.

   Some things have nothing to do with the gift of faith.

   • **The gift of faith is different than the faith needed for salvation.** The gift of faith is received only after salvation.

   > *"⁸For by grace you have been saved through faith, and that not of yourselves; it is the gift of God."*
   > *Ephesians 2.8*

   The faith needed for salvation is a gift given by God to the sinner. It opens the door for anyone to receive Jesus. The gift of faith given by the Holy Spirit empowers believers to work miracles. Faith for salvation acts according to God's plan in the fulfillment of His promises. Faith for miracles operates in the unexpected.

   • The gift of faith is different than overall faith or the "measure of faith."

- God gives all believers a measure of faith to receive your promises; the gift of faith is not given to everyone.

"³For I say, through the grace given to me, to everyone who is among you, not to think of himself more highly than he ought to think, but to think soberly, as God has dealt to each one a measure of faith." Romans 12.3

Although the gift of faith and faith "produce" miracles, the gift of miracles **makes** the miracle happen and the gift of faith **receives** the miracle.

- The gift of faith is different than the fruit of the Spirit called faith.

"²²But the fruit of the Spirit is love, joy, peace, longsuffering, kindness, goodness, faithfulness." Galatians 5.22

The gift of faith is the greatest of the gifts of power.

An example how the gift of faith operates:

"²¹Then Daniel said to the king, "O king, live forever! ²²My God sent His angel and shut the lions' mouths, so that they have not hurt me, because I was found innocent before Him; and also, O king, I have done no wrong before you." ²³Now the king was exceedingly glad for him, and commanded that they should take Daniel up out of the den. So Daniel was taken up out of the den, and no injury whatever was found on him, because he believed in his God." Daniel 6.21-23

What is the purpose for the gift of faith?

- Personal protection during dangerous situations.

> *"³But when Paul had gathered a bundle of sticks and laid them on the fire, a viper came out because of the heat, and fastened on his hand. ⁴So when the natives saw the creature hanging from his hand, they said to one another, "No doubt this man is a murderer, whom, though he has escaped the sea, yet justice does not allow to live." ⁵But he shook off the creature into the fire and suffered no harm." Acts 28.3-5*

- To receive supernatural provisions.

> *"²Then the word of the LORD came to him, saying, ³"Get away from here and turn eastward, and hide by the Brook Cherith, which flows into the Jordan. ⁴And it will be that you shall drink from the brook, and I have commanded the ravens to feed you there." ⁵So he went and did according to the word of the LORD, for he went and stayed by the Brook Cherith, which flows into the Jordan. ⁶The ravens brought him bread and meat in the morning, and bread and meat in the evening; and he drank from the brook." 1 Kings 17.2-6*

- To impart spiritual discipline.

Those individuals who have committed grave offenses are disciplined through the gift of faith. This is what happened with the young men who mocked Elisha. When Elisha disciplined them, two female bears ate them.

"²³Then he went up from there to Bethel; and as he was going up the road, some youths came from the city and mocked him, and said to him, "Go up, you baldhead! Go up, you baldhead!" ²⁴So he turned around and looked at them, and pronounced a curse on them in the name of the LORD. And two female bears came out of the woods and mauled forty-two of the youths." 2 Kings 2.23, 24

- To win battles supernaturally.

"¹⁰So Joshua did as Moses said to him, and fought with Amalek. And Moses, Aaron, and Hur went up to the top of the hill. ¹¹And so it was, when Moses held up his hand, that Israel prevailed; and when he let down his hand, Amalek prevailed."
Exodus 17.10, 11

"³⁰By faith the walls of Jericho fell down after they were encircled for seven days." Hebrews 11.30

- To raise the dead.

Many people were raised from the dead in the Old and New Testament. This is a demonstration of the gift of faith and miracles operating in those days.

- To deliver people from unclean spirits.

"¹¹Now God worked unusual miracles by the hands of Paul, ¹²so that even handkerchiefs or aprons were brought from his body to the sick, and the diseases left them and the evil spirits went out of them."
Acts 19.11, 12

- To provide for financial needs.

  "⁵So she went from him and shut the door behind her and her sons, who brought the vessels to her; and she poured it out. ⁶Now it came to pass, when the vessels were full, that she said to her son, "Bring me another vessel." And he said to her, "There is not another vessel." So the oil ceased. ⁷Then she came and told the man of God. And he said, "Go, sell the oil and pay your debt; and you and your sons live on the rest."
  2 Kings 4.5-7

What is the evidence that proves you have the gift of faith?

- You have an incredible ability to believe the Word of God and His promises.

- You continually believe in physical and financial miracles or any other kind of miracle, whether it is for you or someone else. These miracles happen when you pray for them.

- When other people doubt that miracles can happen, you continue to believe because you have the gift of faith, regardless of the circumstances.

- You always believe that great things can happen, regardless of how much faith is demanded or even if your human ability is not enough to accomplish it.

- You always have a positive, faith-filled attitude. You constantly encourage those around you.

2. **The Gift of Healing.** What is the gift of healing? It is the supernatural manifestation of the Holy Spirit given to a believer to heal all types of diseases, whether they are organic, nervous or mental.

The gift of healing is completely under the control of the Holy Spirit. It operates without human or natural help.

An example of how it operates:

"¹When He had come down from the mountain, great multitudes followed Him. ²And behold, a leper came and worshiped Him, saying, 'Lord, if You are willing, You can make me clean'. ³Then Jesus put out His hand and touched him, saying, 'I am willing; be cleansed'. Immediately his leprosy was cleansed. ⁴And Jesus said to him, 'See that you tell no one; but go your way, show yourself to the priest, and offer the gift that Moses commanded, as a testimony to them'." Matthew 8.1-4

What is the purpose for the gift of healing?

- To heal the sick and destroy the works of the enemy.

   "³⁸...how God anointed Jesus of Nazareth with the Holy Spirit and with power, who went about doing good and healing all who were oppressed by the devil, for God was with Him." Acts 10.38

- To confirm the message of the gospel.

   "²⁸...to do whatever Your hand and Your purpose determined before to be done. ²⁹Now, Lord, look on their threats, and grant to Your servants that with all boldness they may speak Your word, ³⁰by stretching out Your hand

to heal, and that signs and wonders may be done through the name of Your holy Servant Jesus." Acts 4.28-30

We live in a world without God, faith or hope. Because of this, we must preach the gospel with miracles, healing and wonders. If someone doesn't believe through the Word of God, he will believe by works.

- Healing is God's way of advertising.

Every time God wants people to gather together in a particular place, He will perform great miracles and healings.

- The gift of healing gives the glory to God.

"12 Immediately he arose, took up the bed, and went out in the presence of them all, so that all were amazed and glorified God, saying, "We never saw anything like this!" Mark 2.12

How can you minister the gift of healing to the sick?

- By the laying on of hands.

"40 When the sun was setting, all those who had any that were sick with various diseases brought them to Him; and He laid His hands on every one of them and healed them." Luke 4.40

- By the spoken word.

"8 The centurion answered and said, "Lord, I am not worthy that You should come under my roof. But

only speak a word, and my servant will be healed."
Matthew 8.8

What is the most common evidence that proves you have the gift of healing?

• You have great passion to see the sick be healed.

• You have great compassion for the sick.

• You continually pray for people who are sick. Many of these people are healed instantly or progressively.

• Sick people in need of prayer are constantly approaching you.

The gift of healing compliments the evangelistic ministry.

What steps are needed to operate in the gift of healing?

• **Compassion.** Most miracles performed by Jesus were done because of His compassion. Compassion is an important step needed to operate in the gift of healing. It is experiencing someone else's pain and doing something about it.

"35Then Jesus went about all the cities and villages, teaching in their synagogues, preaching the gospel of the kingdom, and healing every sickness and every disease among the people. 36But when He saw the multitudes, He was moved with compassion for them, because they were weary and scattered, like sheep having no shepherd."
Matthew 9.35, 36

- **Faith.** Don't lay hands on people who live in doubt. Only lay hands on the people that believe. This way, God can do something in that person.

How can you activate the gift of healing?

- Begin to pray for the sick right now. Wherever you go or where you are, pray for them. Jesus gave you the great commission of going throughout the world preaching the gospel to all creatures and in His name to heal the sick.

- Ask God to give you the opportunity to pray for a sick person everyday.

- Earnestly desire the gift of healing wholeheartedly, and act upon it all the time.

- Don't be discouraged when you don't see immediate results. Remember that healing can be instantaneous or progressive. Your job is only to believe the Word of God and pray for those who are sick.

- Look for a man or woman of God who operates in the gift of healing and ask him to activate you in this gift.

- Keep a record of the people you pray for and keep count of the ones who receive their healing.

The gift of healing is **not**…

- The prayer that is said over the sick while anointing them with oil. That type of prayer does not necessarily fall under the category of gift of healing.

The gift of healing is not necessarily in operation simply because the elders of a church pray for people and anoint them with oil. The gift of healing is based on the believer's faith and on God's promises.

- To operate in the gift of healing is not the same as praying for the sick. Believers are instructed by Jesus to pray for the sick. He gives them authority to pray for them and gives them His full support. They can pray for the people's faith to increase, but this doesn't necessarily mean that they have the gift of healing.

3. **The Gift of Miracles.** What is the gift of miracles? It is the supernatural manifestation of the Holy Spirit given to a believer. It is the ability to intervene in a supernatural way during the ordinary course of nature or life. It is also a temporary suspension of the natural order of things.

"10...to another the working of miracles, to another prophecy, to another discerning of spirits, to another different kinds of tongues, to another the interpretation of tongues."
1 Corinthians 12.10

What is a miracle?

It is a sudden act of God. It is when God goes outside the natural order to which His creatures and creation are used to living in.

An example of this is Joshua; he ordered the sun and the moon to stop.

"12Then Joshua spoke to the LORD in the day when the LORD delivered up the Amorites before the children of

Israel, and he said in the sight of Israel. "Sun, stand still over Gibeon; And Moon, in the Valley of Aijalon." [13]*So the sun stood still, And the moon stopped, Till the people had revenge Upon their enemies." Joshua 10.12, 13*

You need to keep in mind that a miracle might be of a physical or financial nature. It might be a miracle having to do with health, the transformation of an individual or a door opening where there was no way out, and more.

The difference between the gift of miracles and the gift of healing is that when the miracle occurs, God creates something new, while in the gift of healing He restores something that was damaged.

What is the purpose for the gift of miracles?

• To deliver people from the enemy.

God delivered His people from the bondage of Egypt. In the middle of the dessert, He provided shade, water, food, clothing and more. The Israelites left Egypt with gold and silver. If God can do this, He can also stop trains, guide automobiles, avoid accidents, change the path of a hurricane and avoid earthquakes. He does all these to save His people.

• To provide for those who are needy.

[14]For thus says the LORD God of Israel: "The bin of flour shall not be used up, nor shall the jar of oil run dry, until the day the LORD sends rain on the earth."' [15]So she went away and did according to the word of Elijah; and she and he and her household ate for many days. [16]The

bin of flour was not used up, nor did the jar of oil run dry, according to the word of the LORD which He spoke by Elijah." 1 King 17.14-16

- To confirm the spoken Word.

"¹¹And now, indeed, the hand of the Lord is upon you, and you shall be blind, not seeing the sun for a time." And immediately a dark mist fell on him, and he went around seeking someone to lead him by the hand. ¹²Then the proconsul believed, when he saw what had been done, being astonished at the teaching of the Lord." Acts 13.11, 12

- To deliver us from dangerous situations.

"²³ Now when He got into a boat, His disciples followed Him. ²⁴And suddenly a great tempest arose on the sea, so that the boat was covered with the waves. But He was asleep. ²⁵Then His disciples came to Him and awoke Him, saying, "Lord, save us! We are perishing!" ²⁶But He said to them, "Why are you fearful, O you of little faith?" Then He arose and rebuked the winds and the sea, and there was a great calm." Matthew 8.23-26

- To raise up the dead.

"³⁸Then Jesus, again groaning in Himself, came to the tomb. It was a cave, and a stone lay against it. ³⁹Jesus said, "Take away the stone." Martha, the sister of him who was dead, said to Him, "Lord, by this time there is a stench, for he has been dead four days." ⁴⁰Jesus said to her, "Did I not say to you that if you would believe you would see the glory of God?" ⁴¹Then they took away the stone from the place where the dead man was lying.

And Jesus lifted up His eyes and said, "Father, I thank You that You have heard Me. [42]And I know that You always hear Me, but because of the people who are standing by I said this, that they may believe that You sent Me."[43]Now when He had said these things, He cried with a loud voice, "Lazarus, come forth!" [44]And he who had died came out bound hand and foot with graveclothes, and his face was wrapped with a cloth. Jesus said to them, "Loose him, and let him go." John 11.38-44

- To create new organs.

  [6]When He had said these things, He spat on the ground and made clay with the saliva; and He anointed the eyes of the blind man with the clay. [7]And He said to him, "Go, wash in the pool of Siloam" (which is translated, Sent). So he went and washed, and came back seeing." John 9.6, 7

What evidence proves that you have the gift of miracles?

- You have the gift of faith.

  We are not talking about ordinary faith, but a special kind of faith that believes God for anything.

- God uses you regularly to perform all type of miracles on other people.

- You have seen God perform miracles on the body, miracles having to do with finances, a person's character, and more.

HOW TO HEAR THE VOICE OF GOD
HOW TO HEAR THE VOICE OF GOD

- You have great boldness and assertiveness to pray for things that seem impossible for the human mind to comprehend.

- God answers your prayers with miraculous results.

comfort and courage. Many people call them-selves prophets, but the only words that cons-tantly come from their mouths are words of destruction and death. Don't listen to those kinds of prophecies; do not receive them because they don't come from God and are not in line with His Word.

- **To comfort the church.** The word "comfort" means to bring relief during times of trials and tribulation. Sometimes you might experience dif-ficult situations, but God knows what your con-dition is, and He will give you a prophetic Word to comfort you. You will feel God's embrace and His assurance that He is with you all the time.

- **The believers learn.** This means that believers learn to operate in the gifts of the Spirit. A deep passion to know and understand the supernatural will be activated in them. When the gift of pro-phecy is manifested, you learn about prophecy and also about the rest of the gifts of the Spirit.

"³¹For you can all prophesy one by one, that all may learn and all may be encouraged." 1 Corinthians 14.31

- **To convince the unbelievers.** For example, an unsaved person walks into a church and is approached by a member who gives him a pro-phetic word concerning his life. Things that only he would know are revealed. When this indi-vidual hears these words, unveiling the hidden secrets of his heart, he receives the conviction to repent from sin and invites Jesus to be his Lord and Savior. Now is the time for the church to manifest the supernatural nature of God. This encourages the unbeliever to look for a church that can answer his questions instead of looking into demonic sources for answers. Through you, God reveals His heart.

The gift of prophecy is not...

- The gift of prophecy is not preaching the Word of God. Preaching is speaking Biblical truths that have been thoroughly researched and studied. Prophecy is an improvisation, by inspiration, of the Holy Spirit. Preaching declares the *"logos"*, the written Word. Prophecy proclaims the *"rhema"*, a living word given by God at a specific moment, to a specific individual or group. This gift is not used to guide believers in a certain direction, but to confirm the will of God for their lives.

- The gift of prophecy is not a gift that constantly declares that something bad is about to happen. Some people have been mislead into believing that prophecy only reveals the bad stuff, judgment, or God's condemnation against the people. In truth, this gift is used to edify, encourage and comfort His people.

- The gift of prophecy is not the same as the office of the prophet. Any believer can prophesy, but not every believer is a prophet. The gift of prophecy is given to the individual and the prophet is given to the church.

The Prophetic Personality

W hat are the characteristics of an individual who has the prophetic personality? Before we go into the spiritual characteristics of a person with the prophetic gift, we will learn the visible evidence that proves a believer has the prophetic personality.

- **They have the need to express their thoughts and ideas in a verbal or spiritual manner in reference to what is right or wrong.** Let us see what Paul has to say on this matter:

"22Men of Israel, hear these words: Jesus of Nazareth, a Man attested by God to you by miracles, wonders, and signs which God did through Him in your midst, as you yourselves also know--23Him, being delivered by the determined purpose and foreknowledge of God, you have taken by lawless hands, have crucified, and put to death." Acts 2. 22-23

- **They have the ability to discern when a person is a hypocrite and have a tendency to react very strongly against them.** People with a prophetic personality know how to differentiate between right and wrong, between good and evil. There are no gray areas as far as they are concerned.

"3But Peter said, "Ananias, why has Satan filled your heart to lie to the Holy Spirit and keep back part of the price of the land for yourself? 4While it remained, was it not your own? And after it was sold, was it not in your own control? Why have you conceived this thing in your heart? You have not lied to men but to God." Acts 5.3-4

- **People with a prophetic personality are very impulsive.** Regardless of the cost to their personal life, they will react at a moment's notice to see that justice is done.

  "⁶Then He came to Simon Peter. And Peter said to Him, "Lord, are You washing my feet?" ⁷Jesus answered and said to him, "What I am doing you do not understand now, but you will know after this." ⁸Peter said to Him, "You shall never wash my feet!" Jesus answered him, "If I do not wash you, you have no part with Me." ⁹Simon Peter said to Him, "Lord, not my feet only, but also my hands and my head!" ¹⁰Jesus said to him, "He who is bathed needs only to wash his feet, but is completely clean; and you are clean, but not all of you." John 13.6-10

- **They are willing to suffer to do what is right.** Regardless of what it takes or the consequences that may arise, they hold firm to their decisions for as long as it takes truth to prevail.

  "²⁹But Peter and the other apostles answered and said: "We ought to obey God rather than men." Acts 5. 29

- **They are direct, persuasive and assertive.** People with a prophetic personality never run out of things to say. They are bold and honest when they speak. They don't mince words, but speak the truth face to face.

- **They hate what is wrong.** People with a prophetic personality have the divine ability to identify what is wrong and to confront the situation immediately. They are able to sense when something is wrong in different situations and in people.

They can't tolerate this. Their greatest desire is to see God exalted. Because they hate injustice; they might even take the initiative to defend anyone who is wrongfully accused.

- **They know how to love and how to be faithful friends.** People who operate in the prophetic, truly love God and the people. When they decide to be a friend, they are faithful and loyal until death.

- **They are quick to judge, quick to speak and quick to act before thinking.** Sometimes their judgments are based on what they see or hear. They react too quickly. They don't take a moment to think before accusing or judging another person.

"¹⁰Then Simon Peter, having a sword, drew it and struck the high priest's servant, and cut off his right ear. The servant's name was Malchus. ¹¹So Jesus said to Peter, "Put your sword into the sheath. Shall I not drink the cup which My Father has given Me?" John 18.10, 11

- **They have strict and rigid convictions and beliefs.** They see everything as good or bad, true or false, right or wrong, black or white. They have no gray areas. They do not compromise their beliefs. Their logo is, "Do it now and do it right."

What are some of the problems encountered by the people who have a prophetic personality?

- The truth, as they see it, might offend and hurt people.

- Because of their convictions, they are not flexible. They can easily develop a blind spot in their life because of their opinions.

- They cut themselves off from people who sin. When they see someone living in sin, their tendency is to cut them off. If they are not careful, these people might be lost forever.

- They condemn themselves when they fail God. They judge themselves as strongly and as harshly as they judge others.

- They have a tendency to discipline the people who are not under their responsibility. You must remember that you do not have the right to discipline anyone unless you have a relationship with that person. People with a prophetic personality tend to discipline and correct everybody because they hate sin.

When you receive a prophetic word to discipline anyone, ask the Lord's permission whether to do it right away or if you should wait for a later time; this is godly wisdom. You need it to operate in the prophetic.

- They perceive the negative more than the positive. They are more sensitive to what is bad instead of what is good. People with the prophetic personality must protect themselves from the danger of going against people or things instead of granting them favor.

What is the spiritual evidence that proves you have the gift of prophecy?

- You possess great spiritual sensitivity.

- You quickly perceive what is good or bad regardless of where you are or whom you are with.

- You are passionate about building up the brokenhearted. Remember that the gift of prophecy is used to encourage, comfort and edify. Because of this gift, you will feel the desire to strengthen the weak, comfort the brokenhearted, to encourage and edify the church of Christ.

- You are often used by God to give prophetic words to people in need of encouragement. God will allow you to see, feel and to hear things about other people when you least expect it or before you have the opportunity to ask God about it.

- The prophecies you have declared in previous occasions have come to pass.

- You love the supernatural. Everything that is prophetic is supernatural. Therefore, if you have the gift of prophecy, you have great passion for the supernatural, miracles, healings, signs and wonders. These are only a few examples; there are too many to mention.

What things should you understand concerning personal prophecy?

- **Personal prophecy is only partial.** The spoken word given through the gift of prophecy is only a small portion of the knowledge and wisdom of God concerning future things. The gift of prophecy is only a small demonstration or revelation of the will of God. God doesn't reveal your entire life at once, but He will reveal small portions to help you act and walk by faith.

  "For we know in part and we prophesy in part."
  1 Corinthians 13.9

- **Personal prophecy is progressive.** All personal prophecies are progressively fulfilled throughout the years. As God reveals His perfect will to you, you will be able to see the whole picture.

- **Personal prophecy is conditional.** The outcome of personal prophecy depends on the individual who receives it. The reason many people die before their personal prophecy is fulfilled is because they disobeyed what God asked them to do through the prophecy they received. There are divine prophecies that are unconditional, including divine declarations that are irrevocable. These will surely be fulfilled at any given time and there is no one who can stop them from becoming a reality. These are usually general prophecies and not personal ones. Personal prophecy is conditional on the individual's obedience. If he does not obey, the prophecy will not come to pass.

For example, God spoke to a businessman revealing to him that he was going to receive millions of dollars to bless the Kingdom of God. However, as he waited for his prophecy to come true; he didn't tithe or give any offerings from what he already had. In other words, He didn't sow anything into the kingdom; he did not act upon the word; he disobeyed God. If this person does not change his stingy mentality and continues to act like this, the prophetic word from God that said he would receive millions of dollars will never be fulfilled in his life.

What are unconditional prophecies?

Unconditional prophecies have to do with the overall and universal plans and purposes of God for humanity. No one can stop these prophecies from coming to pass. They have been declared by God and will come to pass regardless of what is happening. God said it and that settles it.

What are conditional prophecies?

Conditional prophecies are prophetic words given by God to specific individuals. These may or may not come to pass; they can be cancelled or eliminated if the individual does not obey.

Every prophecy must be judged in the congregation by at least two or three people. Remember that only the prophecy is judged not the prophet. At times, even though a prophet is not living a righteous life, he is still able to bring an exact and precise prophetic word. There are many examples of this found in the Bible. The prophet is not categorized by the precision of his prophecy, but by the maturity of his character. In other words, the fruit of the Spirit in his life.

Prophecy is judged according to the following criteria:

• Every personal prophecy must be in line with the written Word of God.

> *"¹⁹And so we have the prophetic word confirmed, which you do well to heed as a light that shines in a dark place, until the day dawns and the morning star rises in your hearts; ²⁰knowing this first, that no prophecy of Scripture is of any private interpretation, ²¹for prophecy never came by the will of man, but holy men of God spoke as they were moved by the Holy Spirit." 2 Peter 1.19-21*

For example, there are people who say, "God said I should leave my wife and marry someone else." This contradicts the Word of God. Therefore, it should be disregarded.

Some people use the prophetic gift to manipulate and control other people. They even perform wedding ceremonies or appoint people into the ministry when in truth their prophecies were the result of their own flesh. Samuel calls this kind of prophecies the sin of witchcraft.

You should walk in the Spirit and enjoy a close relationship with God so that you may be influenced by the Holy Spirit and not by your flesh or by demonic spirits of divination.

There are three sources of inspiration when you prophesy:

- A demonic spirit
- The human spirit
- The Spirit of God

- Every prophecy must be in harmony with the testimony of the Holy Spirit. If a prophecy contradicts the testimony of the Holy Spirit, then it is better to disregard it.

- Prophecy produces the fruit of the Spirit. When God uses anybody to give you a prophetic word, it increases your love, peace and patience. It makes you kinder, and it increases and strengthens your faith. This is a sign that the prophetic word came from God.

- Two or three people should confirm every personal prophecy. It is wise to get this confirmation before making a decision based on the prophecy, thus confirming what the Word says, "Let others judge."

"29Let two or three prophets speak, and let the others judge."
1 Corinthians 14.29

What should you do when you receive a prophecy?

There are people who say, "If this prophecy is from God, it will come to pass. I will hang the prophecy on the wall and if it doesn't come to pass, then it was not from God." This is the wrong attitude to have. For a prophecy to come to pass, you must do your part.

What should you do?

- **Respond in faith.** After you receive the prophetic word, begin to act on what the Spirit is asking you to do. He will guide you to do the corresponding action, thus making it possible for the prophecy to come to pass

  "But without faith it is impossible to please Him, for he who comes to God must believe that He is, and that He is a rewarder of those who diligently seek Him." Hebrews 11.6

- **Obey God.** True faith goes hand in hand with obedience. Obedience is dependent upon two things: hearing and doing. If you hear the prophecy, but don't act according to what you heard, the prophetic word will not come to pass.

  "²²But be doers of the word, and not hearers only, deceiving yourselves." James 1.22

  It is better not to know, than to know and do nothing about it.

- **Patience is very important.** One definition for the word "patience" is to remain encouraged in the midst of difficulty. Sometimes you need a great deal of patience to wait for God's promises. The more difficult the situations in your life, the more patience you are going to need as you wait. If you are not patient, it could cause you to abort the plan of God for your life. Impatience also opens the door for the enemy to present you with an Ishmael before your Isaac arrives.

"ᵈNow Sarai, Abram's wife, had borne him no children. And she had an Egyptian maidservant whose name was Hagar." Genesis 16.1

This is what happened to Abraham and Sarai. After waiting twelve years for God's Word to come to pass, they became impatient. Sarai, Abram's wife, suggested he should take her servant, Hagar; a proposition which he quickly accepted. The result of their impatience and disobedience was the birth of Ishmael. The Bible calls him a wild man or, literally, a "wild beast." The consequences of Abraham's disobedience are still felt today as we hear of the problems between the Muslims (Ishmael's descendants) and the Jews.

"ᵈ¹And the Angel of the LORD said to her: "Behold, you are with child, and you shall bear a son. You shall call his name Ishmael, because the LORD has heard your affliction. ¹²He shall be a wild man; His hand shall be against every man, and every man's hand against him. And he shall dwell in the presence of all his brethren." Genesis 16.11-12

Abraham's son Isaac came after Ishmael was born. The enemy will always try to bring Ishmael into your life before God brings Isaac, the son of the promise.

"ᵈ²...that you do not become sluggish, but imitate those who through faith and patience inherit the promises." Hebrews 6.12

Wait patiently upon the Lord for He shall fulfill what He promised! Wait upon Him. He will keep His Word. Many marriages, ministers and businesses are the result of decisions taken at a moment when people stopped waiting patiently for God's promises to be fulfilled. Because of their impatience, instead of receiving their "Isaac", what they got was "Ishmael", which only causes division and bickering. The best way to avoid getting what you don't want is to wait on God!

- **Make war with your prophecies.** Every time you receive a prophecy, go to war against the enemy for it. Take hold of it, write it down, meditate on it and remind God of it. There are promises of God for your life and ministry. When the enemy discourages you, remind him of the prophetic words you received.

  "18This charge I commit to you, son Timothy, according to the prophecies previously made concerning you, that by them you may wage the good warfare." 1 Timothy 1.18

- **Grab hold of the prophecy.** It is extremely important that you take hold of your promise immediately after receiving the prophecy.

Why is it important to take hold of the prophecy?

- **It is a reminder for the person who received it.** Sometimes you are under the anointing when you receive the prophecy and if it's long, it will be difficult for you to remember most of it at a later time. This is why you must record it, write it down and meditate on it for your own benefit.

- **It protects the person who gave the prophecy.** Many people misinterpret prophecy. When the prophetic word is taken out of context, bad decisions are made. If the prophecies are written down, the prophet is protected from bad interpretations.

The second gift that is under the gift of inspiration (vocal) is the gift of different kinds of tongues.

1. Different kinds of tongues

What is the gift of different kinds of tongues?

It is the supernatural expression given by the Holy Spirit to speak in other tongues, which have not been learned or that are not understood by the person's natural mind.

Every believer should be able to speak in other tongues. They are personal. The gift of speaking in other tongues is one of the signs Jesus said would follow you. They are given for the edification of the believer and not for the body of Christ. This gift is different from the gift of interpretation of tongues, which is given for the edification of the church.

There is a difference between speaking in tongues as a sign of the baptism of the Holy Spirit and the gift of interpretation of tongues for all believers.

What is the purpose of the gift of tongues as the initial sign to the believer when he receives the baptism of the Holy Spirit?

• To speak in tongues is the Scriptural evidence of the baptism of the Holy Spirit.

"And they were all filled with the Holy Spirit and began to speak with other tongues, as the Spirit gave them utterance." Acts 2.4

- To speak with God in a supernatural way.

  "²For he who speaks in a tongue does not speak to men but to God, for no one understands him; however, in the spirit he speaks mysteries." 1 Corinthians 14. 2

- To magnify God.

  "⁴⁶For they heard them speak with tongues and magnify God." Acts 10. 46

- To edify you.

  "⁴He who speaks in a tongue edifies himself, but he who prophesies edifies the church." I Corinthians 14.4

2. The gift of interpretation of tongues

What is the gift of interpretation of tongues?

It is the supernatural manifestation given by the Holy Spirit to a believer to interpret the message given in an unknown tongue.

What is the main reason the gift of speaking in other tongues is given?

- To edify the church

  "¹²Even so you, since you are zealous for spiritual gifts, let it be for the edification of the church that you seek to excel." 1 Corinthians 14.12

Remember that the gift of interpretation of tongues is not a literal word-by-word translation, but an interpretation of a message given in tongues, whether it is long or short.

How can you discover your spiritual gift?

- **Explore the possibilities.**

  Look for sources that will help you identify what your gift is. Investigate the definition and evidence the gift has to help you operate in it properly.

- **Experiment with different gifts.**

  Ask yourself the following questions:

  Do I have this gift? How often am I used in this gift? When I operate in this gift what are the results? When I am operating in this gift, do I feel happy or frustrated? Have I had a passion for it all my life? Could this be my gift?

  Begin to experiment in the different gifts. Get involved in different ministries in your local church and serve in what you believe to be your gift.

- **Examine your feelings.**

  What do you like the most?

  How does it feel to operate within your gift?

  Ask yourself the following questions: Do I have peace and joy when I do this? Does this gift compliment my personality and temperament? Do I want to do this the rest of my life? Is this what fulfills me the most? If I do something else will I feel empty and alone?

- **Evaluate your effectiveness.**

  Ask yourself: What happens after you operate in the gift? Are the results positive or negative? How often does God use me in this gift?

- **God's confirmation, your spiritual covering and the church.**

  When you genuinely have a gift, God will always back you up with the anointing. Your spiritual covering, which is your mentor or pastor, will recognize the gifts within you. The people will also look for you to confirm it because they will recognize that you have the gift.

Gifts of Revelation

$\mathcal{T}$ hrough the gifts of revelation God reveals something specific to His people.

It is very important to know what the gifts of revelation are, and to understand them. If you desire to walk in the prophetic, you will see these gifts operating in you.

1. Words of Science or Knowledge.

What is the gift of word of science?

The word of science or knowledge is the supernatural revelation of the Holy Spirit given at a specific moment to reveal certain things that are in the mind of God, and hidden truths having to do with the past or present, people, places or things. His revelation can only come about in a supernatural way.

The gift of the word of science or knowledge is not...

- The gift of knowledge, but the gift of the word knowledge.
- Knowledge that can be obtained through the learning process.
- Knowledge that is accumulated in a lifetime.

There are three levels of knowledge:

- **Human or natural knowledge.** This kind of knowledge is acquired throughout a lifetime of personal experiences and teachings.

- **Biblical knowledge.** This kind of knowledge is acquired through reading, studying and meditating on the Word of God.

- **The gift of science or knowledge.** This kind of gift from the Holy Spirit comes at a specific moment through supernatural revelation. This knowledge has nothing to do with natural or biblical understanding; it is a revelation of the Holy Spirit.

What is the purpose for the gift of the word of science?

- **To reveal the enemy's plans.**

   "12 And one of his servants said, 'None, my lord, O king; but Elisha, the prophet who is in Israel, tells the king of Israel the words that you speak in your bedroom'." 2 Kings 6.12

- **To reveal hidden sin.**

   "26 Then he said to him, 'Did not my heart go with you when the man turned back from his chariot to meet you? Is it time to receive money and to receive clothing, olive groves and vineyards, sheep and oxen, male and female servants? 27 Therefore the leprosy of Naaman shall cling to you and your descendants forever.' And he went out from his presence leprous, as white as snow." 2 Kings 5.26-27

- **To reveal the reason for sickness or demonic influence.** Sometimes God reveals the reason why a person is sick. Other times, God reveals the reason why the person can't be delivered from satanic oppression.

- **To reveal things concerning lost people, things or property.** The Word of God tells about the time that Saul's donkeys were lost. The prophet Samuel revealed to Saul that the donkeys were safe and that they had been found.

"[20]But as for your donkeys that were lost three days ago, do not be anxious about them, for they have been found. And on whom is all the desire of Israel? Is it not on you and on all your father's house." 1 Samuel 9.20

If there is something missing in your life, ask the Lord to reveal it to you. It doesn't matter what you have lost, whether it is a person, or anything of great value to you; simply ask God and He will show you the way.

Illustration: My gold chain.

My family and I were vacationing in Fort Myers. As we were preparing to leave the hotel, I noticed my gold chain was missing. I returned to the hotel room and looked around for it. I must have spent at least twenty minutes trying to find it without success. After my fruitless effort, I asked the Lord where it was. Instantly, I received an impression of where the chain was. It was hidden in the back of a drawer in one of the hotel rooms. I went directly to that drawer and there it was. Praise God!

- **To reveal people's secrets.** This gift reveals the hidden secrets of the heart. It brings correction, repentance and spiritual benefit. God will often reveal specific things concerning an individual to motivate him to change his lifestyle, to bring him to repentance and to bless him.

- **To reveal the root of the problem and the solution.** God will reveal the reason why something is happening and the answer to the problems relating to deliverance, healing and counseling. When a person is receiving counseling, it is because there is usually a deeply rooted problem. It is so deep that even the person seeking the counseling is unaware of it. The guidance of the Holy Spirit is very important at this time because the cause of the problem and the solution to it needs to be revealed before the individual can receive the answers he is looking for.

- **To reveal a strategy on how to pray for a specific situation.** When you pray for a specific situation, the Holy Spirit will reveal to you a strategy on how to penetrate and do spiritual warfare against the situation at hand.

- **To reveal sin and corruption in an individual.**

"¹But a certain man named Ananias, with Sapphira his wife, sold a possession. ²And he kept back part of the proceeds, his wife also being aware of it, and brought a certain part and laid it at the apostles' feet. ³But Peter said, "Ananias, why has Satan filled your heart to lie to the Holy Spirit and keep back part of the price of the land for yourself? ⁴While it remained, was it not your own? And after it was sold, was it not in your own control? Why have you conceived this thing in your heart? You have not lied to men but to God." ⁵Then Ananias, hearing these words, fell down and breathed his last. So great fear came upon all those who heard these things. ⁶And the young men arose and wrapped him up, carried him out, and buried him. ⁷Now it was about three hours

later when his wife came in, not knowing what had happened. [8]And Peter answered her, "Tell me whether you sold the land for so much?" She said, "Yes, for so much." [9]Then Peter said to her, "How is it that you have agreed together to test the Spirit of the Lord? Look, the feet of those who have buried your husband are at the door, and they will carry you out." [10]Then immediately she fell down at his feet and breathed her last. And the young men came in and found her dead, and carrying her out, buried her by her husband." Acts 5.1-10

- **To reveal hidden things in the life of an individual.**

[15]The woman said to Him, "Sir, give me this water, that I may not thirst, nor come here to draw." [16]Jesus said to her, "Go, call your husband, and come here." [17]The woman answered and said, "I have no husband." Jesus said to her, "You have well said, "I have no husband,' [18]for you have had five husbands, and the one whom you now have is not your husband; in that you spoke truly." [19]The woman said to Him, "Sir, I perceive that You are a prophet." John 4.15-19

The word of science has the ability to penetrate through all human appearances. It is a supernatural ability given by God to a believer.

How can you operate in the gift of the word of science or knowledge?

- **By inspiration or motivation from the Holy Spirit.**

It is impossible for you to possess this supernatural gift unless the Holy Spirit gives it to you.

- **It must be activated by faith.**

  When God reveals something about a person or thing, you must step out in faith and share what God has revealed. This is how the gift is activated.

What is the evidence that proves you have the gift of the word of science or knowledge?

- **When God reveals to you past or present things about an individual, and he does it often.** The key to having this gift is for God to show you specific situations concerning individuals such as: marriage, health or finances. Sometimes, God will reveal the sin that someone has committed in the past and also in the present. Other times, God will reveal the hidden motives and intentions of the heart of the other person to protect us. Many times, you will suddenly receive a specific word of knowledge about a person you were not even thinking about. Sometimes, it will happen frequently. If this is your situation, then it means you have this gift.

- **When God is constantly showing you the enemy's plans and strategies against yourself or someone else.** Sometimes you will be able to discern, which spirit is tormenting a person, how it entered into his life and the solution to deliver that person from demonic oppression. At other times, you will enter a particular home and God will reveal to you satanic objects that are giving legal rights to the enemy to remain in that home.

Remember that if you have the gift, God will often reveal things to you concerning people, places, things, dangers and decisions you must make. The gift operates in such a simple way that it is unnecessary to be asking God to reveal things to you. In some believers the gift of word of knowledge operates stronger than in others; this is due to the call of God upon that person. Prophets are usually the ones who operate in this gift.

2. **The gift of the word of wisdom.**

What is the gift of word of wisdom?

It is the supernatural revelation given by the Holy Spirit to a person at a specific moment. Through this gift, the Holy Spirit reveals the mind, will and purpose of God for His people and the events that are about to happen in their future.

"8...for to one is given the word of wisdom through the Spirit, to another the word of knowledge through the same Spirit."
1 Corinthians 12.8

What the gift of the word of wisdom is not...

• This gift is not called the gift of wisdom, but the gift of the **word** of wisdom.

• It is not human wisdom acquired in a lifetime.

• It is not divine wisdom acquired through years of studying the Bible.

Three levels of wisdom:

Human or natural wisdom. This kind of wisdom is acquired through good and bad experiences.

Divine or Biblical wisdom. The Word of God gives you the ability to acquire wisdom for each area of your life such as family, finances, friends and more.

The gift of the word of wisdom. This gift of the Holy Spirit reveals God's will concerning future events. The word of science and the word of wisdom complement each other. One reveals situations and events from the past and present, and the other reveals situations concerning future events. When the prophetic word concerning the future is given, it is sometimes followed by a word of wisdom. Some people label everything a prophecy, but remember that there are nine gifts in operation.

What is the purpose of the gift of wisdom?

- **To warn of future dangers and avoid suffering the consequences.**

   "[12]Then, being divinely warned in a dream that they should not return to Herod, they departed for their own country another way." Mathew 2.12

   God will reveal future dangers so you can take the necessary precautions and not fall in the trap of the enemy.

- **To announce that judgments and blessings are on their way.**

    "¹²Then the men said to Lot, "Have you anyone else here? Son-in-law, your sons, your daughters, and whomever you have in the city--take them out of this place!¹³For we will destroy this place, because the outcry against them has grown great before the face of the LORD, and the LORD has sent us to destroy it." Genesis 19.12-13

- **To confirm and reveal a divine appointment.**

    Sometimes God will give you a word of wisdom to share with you His will and purpose concerning a divine appointment for someone else.

- **To confirm blessings that are on their way.**

    Sometimes you lose heart in regards to the promises of God, but through the word of wisdom He assures you that the promises will be fulfilled.

How to operate in the gift of word of wisdom:

- **By inspiration or motivation of the Holy Spirit.**

    The Holy Spirit gives you the ability to know the positive and negative aspects of the people.

- **When we are activated by faith.**

    All things concerning God are done and activated by faith. The gift of words of wisdom is also activated by faith.

What is the evidence that proves you have the gift of the word of wisdom?

- When God constantly reveals to you things and plans about people and their future.

- When God constantly reveals to you dangers, blessings and future judgment about people or nations.

- When God reveals and confirms His blessings operating in a person.

If you have never operated in the gift of the word of wisdom, then begin to do it today and the Lord will honor your faith.

3. **The gift of discernment of spirits.**

What is the gift of discernment of spirits?

It is the supernatural ability given to a person by the Holy Spirit to understand, perceive and see which spirits are oppressing a person or place. The person with this gift has the ability to penetrate the spiritual world and recognize the spirits that are good and those that are bad.

The gift of discernment of spirits includes the following four aspects:

- *Understands* how spirits operate.
- *Perceives* when the spirits are active.
- *Recognizes* spirits.
- *Sees* spirits.

The gift of discernment of spirits is not…

- Reading people's minds and thoughts.
- Revealing the sin in people.
- Only seeing demons.

Many people claim to have the gift of discernment of spirits, but the only thing they seem to see is what is bad. This gift is useful to identify different types of spirits, the good and the bad.

There are three levels of discernment:

Natural discernment. God created humanity with a spirit and every human being has a certain level of natural perception that is given by God. Although man sinned, he still has the ability to perceive things in the spirit realm.

Psychic discernment. This kind of discernment has to do with the soul of the individual. Perception has to do with the mind and the emotions.

Spiritual discernment or discernment of spirits. This covers many areas such as properly judging what is in the heart of man or perceiving the presence of evil spirits or good spirits. It also means to have the ability to see beyond the physical realm, to penetrate and see into the spiritual world.

What is the purpose for the gift of discernment of spirits?

- **It delivers** the ones who are oppressed by the enemy.

God will reveal to you the tormenting spirits operating in people. This revelation enables you to deliver them from the enemy's oppression.

"[18]The Spirit of the LORD is upon Me, because He has anointed Me to preach the gospel to the poor; He has sent Me to heal the brokenhearted, to proclaim liberty to the captives and recovery of sight to the blind, to set at liberty those who are oppressed." Luke 4.18

- **It reveals** who serves the devil.

Many Satanists infiltrate the church to harm believers. This is a very important reason why you need to have this gift and to know how to operate in it. You need it to unmask the ones who serve the enemy.

"[11]And now, indeed, the hand of the Lord is upon you, and you shall be blind, not seeing the sun for a time." And immediately a dark mist fell on him, and he went around seeking someone to lead him by the hand. [12]Then the proconsul believed, when he saw what had been done, being astonished at the teaching of the Lord." Acts 13.11-12

- **It exposes** mistakes.

There are spirits assigned to cause people to stumble and make mistakes. These spirits have infiltrated the church and are operating in the body of Christ causing division. Through this gift they can be detected and dealt with.

"Now the Spirit expressly says that in latter times some will depart from the faith, giving heed to deceiving spirits and doctrines of demons." 1 Timothy 4.1

- **It resists** the adversary.

  You can't resist the enemy with your own strength, but you can resist him with the gifts of the Holy Spirit.

- **It reveals the existence** of strongholds and principalities over geological areas.

- **It reveals the direction and the leading of the Holy Spirit for a church service.** Sometimes pastors conduct their church services according to established human agendas. They don't allow the Holy Spirit to guide or speak to them. However, through the application of this gift, you can receive direction from the Holy Spirit.

- **It reveals the intentions and motives of the human spirit.** Jesus was able to detect the motives and intentions of the religious enemies of His time.

How do you know you have the gift of discernment of spirits?

- **Because you often see and perceive the spiritual realm.** Many people operate in this gift. You know you have this gift because God continually reveals to you how other people behave, what kind of spirit is influencing them and occasionally, the Lord allows you to see into the spiritual realm.

- **Because you are extremely sensitive to the spiritual world.** Regardless of where you go, you will be able to see and perceive things in the spiritual realm.

There is a fine line of perception between the natural and the spiritual realm. If you have the gift of discernment of spirits, there is the danger that you might become extremely sensitive to many things (more to the bad stuff than the good); you will perceive everything and feel everything until finally these become a burden.

The gift of discernment of spirits is indispensable for every pastor because many people will approach him and his ministry dressed as angels of light to cause division among his sheep.

CHAPTER V

Five Methods Used to Prophesy

od left you His written Word to speak to you; guide you; discipline and teach you. Any method He chooses to speak to you must adhere itself to His written Word. The written Word of God is above any voice, dream, vision or inner witness. If you receive a word through one of these methods and it doesn't align itself to His written Word, you can't accept it as a prophetic word given by God.

Beyond the written word, God uses five other ways to communicate His prophetic word to you:

1. The ministry of the prophet

The gift of the prophet is not a gift of the Holy Spirit, but an extension of the ministry of Jesus Christ given to the church. The office or the ministry of the prophet has been designated and created to function at a higher level than the gift of prophecy given by the Holy Spirit. The gift of prophecy operates in the saints for the edification, comfort and exhortation of the believers, but the office of the ministry of the prophet was anointed for various other things.

"[11]And He Himself gave some to be apostles, some prophets, some evangelists, and some pastors and teachers." Ephesians 4.11

*"[28]And God has appointed these in the church: first apostles, second prophets, third teachers, after that miracles, then gifts of healings, helps, administrations, varieties of tongues."
1 Corinthians 12.28*

What is a prophet?

A prophet is one who speaks in God's name. He will speak things relating to the past, present or future. In the Old Testament, the prophets are called "seers". A "seer" is one who receives visions and revelations from God. He speaks only when he is suddenly inspired or illuminated to do so by a momentary revelation.

What are the characteristics of a prophet?

- **He operates strongly in the gifts of revelation.**

  Let us review what the gifts of revelations are:

  - Word of science
  - Word of wisdom
  - Discernment of spirit

- A prophet will often have the ability to see in the spiritual realm through the gift of discernment. He has the ability to see dangers and things beyond what others may see. He also has supernatural visions.

- For the most part, prophets operate under another ministry. In other words, besides being prophets they can also be pastors, evangelists or teachers. The prophetic ministry always goes hand in hand with other ministries. There could be combinations such as: prophet/evangelist; prophet/pastor; prophet /teacher or all together: prophet/pastor/teacher/ evangelist. In Dr. Bill Hamon's case, he is an apostle and a prophet.

- There is a great difference between what a prophet is and prophesizing. There is a difference between the office of the prophet and prophecy. Any believer can

136

have the ability to prophesy at a specific moment, but this doesn't make him a prophet. However, all prophets can prophecy all the time. New Testament prophecy is for edifying, comforting and exhorting.

- Prophets bring the **prophetic revelation.**

"⁷Surely the Lord GOD does nothing, unless He reveals His secret to His servants the prophets." Amos 3.7

According to the Word of God, revelations may come in dreams and visions. Prophets are "seers"; they know beforehand the plans and will of God.

- Prophets have great **authority.**

"¹⁰See, I have this day set you over the nations and over the kingdoms, to root out and to pull down, to destroy and to throw down, to build and to plant." Jeremiah 1.10

Prophetic authority gives the prophet the ability to pull out, demolish the roots of demonic strongholds and to destroy all demonic deeds. They also have the authority to plant, sow and edify the Kingdom of God.

- Prophets **activate** the gifts of the Holy Spirit in the people.

"¹⁰So I prophesied as He commanded me, and breath came into them, and they lived, and stood upon their feet, an exceedingly great army." Ezekiel 37.10

The anointing upon a prophet gives him the ability to activate the people. Through their messages they are able to activate gifts and ministries for the believers. When believers are disoriented and spiritually cold, prophets have the anointing to stir them up and to help them find their way back.

- Prophets **confirm the things of God.**

"³²Now Judas and Silas, themselves being prophets also, exhorted and strengthened the brethren with many words." Acts 15.32

God has appointed the prophet's ministry to bring confirmation, to strengthen, to bring assurance and remove any doubt from the hearts and minds of the people. When they confirm a divine appointment, a vision, a word or a decision, the people become stronger, remain constant and continue to grow in the Lord.

- Prophets **help** out in the house of the Lord.

"¹Then the prophet Haggai and Zechariah the son of Iddo, prophets, prophesied to the Jews who were in Judah and Jerusalem, in the name of the God of Israel, who was over them. ²So Zerubbabel the son of Shealtiel and Jeshua the son of Jozadak rose up and began to build the house of God which is in Jerusalem; and the prophets of God were with them, helping them." Ezra 5.1-2

When God begins to do something, somewhere, satanic opposition will always try to rise up against it. Because of this, God sends His prophets to help the local pastors and to enlighten them on how to avoid the attacks of the enemy. The prophet acts like a spiritual radar detecting any plan of the devil.

2. The gift of prophecy

The gift of prophecy is another channel used to prophesy. The word "prophecy" in the Greek language is the word "naba," meaning to bubble up like a spring, to flow forward, to declare something that can only be known through divine revelation.

Prophecy is one of the nine gifts of the Holy Spirit. It is an ability and grace, which is not given because of Christian maturity, but because the Holy Spirit desires to bless the people.

"³¹For you can all prophesy one by one, that all may learn and all may be encouraged." 1 Corinthians 14.31

You have learned about the gift of prophecy and how to operate in this gift, but there are other things you need to learn concerning prophecy.

It is extremely important to seek advice from your spiritual covering. Your pastor or mentor will help you interpret the prophecies. Unfortunately, there are extreme cases when the gift of prophecy was misused for self-benefit.

The Word of God teaches that using prophecy to manipulate other people is equivalent to the sin of witchcraft.

Many people use the gift of prophecy to join two people in matrimony or to appoint someone into the ministry and send them out. Prophecy is also used to gain money, control the will of the people, to convince the believers to join the ministry or to intimidate them. These are only a few reasons why some people use the gift of prophecy. The Word of God calls this the sin of witchcraft. If any of you are practicing this, then you must repent of this sin. However, just because there are some people abusing the gift of prophecy for self-gain, it doesn't mean there aren't genuine prophets who truly love God and want to exalt Jesus and edify God's people.

There are more genuine prophets than false prophets.

If you are a new believer and someone approaches you with a prophecy, but you have doubts about it, go and ask your pastoral covering. Do not make any hasty decisions based on what you hear.

3. **Prophetic preaching**

This is one of the five methods by which someone can prophesy.

As previously stated, preaching and prophecy are not the same thing. To preach is to speak the written Word; to prophesy is to speak by divine inspiration supplying a specific need at that very moment. Prophetic preaching occurs at a different level than normal preaching; it has different qualities.

Characteristics and qualities of prophetic preaching:

- It must be a Biblical truth and aligned with God's Word.

- The words and illustrations given by the preacher are the exact ones God wants to share at that instant.

- The message is specifically directed to the people present at that moment.

- Any believer can operate under prophetic teaching.

One way to describe prophetic teaching would be when I am preaching. As I deliver the word I had previously prepared, I will suddenly deviate from the main subject of the preaching and say, "I am saying this, but I do not understand why I am saying it." Sometimes, the Holy Spirit meets us half way through a sermon to reveal a specific word and at that precise moment to someone in the congregation.

4. The prophetic presbytery

What is a prophetic presbytery?

It is a team of experienced, capable and mature prophets and elders. They are wise and spiritually mature, approved and qualified to minister to the people through the Holy Spirit.

"¹Now in the church that was at Antioch there were certain prophets and teachers: Barnabas, Simeon who was called Niger, Lucius of Cyrene, Manaen who had been brought up with Herod the tetrarch, and Saul. ²As they ministered to the Lord and fasted, the Holy Spirit said, "Now separate to Me Barnabas and Saul for the work to which I have called them." Acts 13.1-2

The prophetic presbytery is another method used to prophesy. When a team of men and women gather together to bring the prophetic word to the people,

141

they can impart gifts from God through the laying on of hands.

Why is a prophetic presbytery needed?

- **To confirm the will of God in the life of an individual.** When this prophetic presbytery joins together, it confirms a divine appointment and the will of God for the believers.

- **To impart spiritual gifts.**

  "[14]Do not neglect the gift that is in you, which was given to you by prophecy with the laying on of the hands of the eldership." I Timothy 4.14

- **To understand the divine appointment, the will of God and your place in the body of Christ.** The prophetic presbytery helps you to know and understand what your calling is and to help you find your place within the body of Christ.

- **To promote growth and spiritual maturity.** After receiving a word from God, you will be edified and encouraged. It will take you to a higher level.

- **To ordain people into the ministry.** When the prophetic presbytery gathers together, it ordains people into the ministry. They confirm your calling and position within the body of Christ. They also activate the gifts of the Holy Spirit in you to begin functioning within God's calling.

"⁶For this reason I left you in Crete, that you should set in order the things that are lacking, and appoint elders in every city as I commanded you." Titus 1.5

5. The spirit of prophecy and prophetic worship.

What is the spirit of prophecy? It is the testimony of Jesus Christ. This is not the gift of prophecy or the office of the prophet, but a special anointing that comes from Jesus and received by you, the believer. Sometimes, the spirit of prophecy descends when a special anointing is present.

"¹⁰And I fell at his feet to worship him. But he said to me, "See that you do not do that! I am your fellow servant, and of your brethren who have the testimony of Jesus. Worship God! For the testimony of Jesus is the spirit of prophecy." Revelation 19.10

The manifestation of the spirit of prophecy comes in two ways:

- **Through worship.** When you worship God through music, the prophetic move is free to operate.

   "¹⁵But now bring me a musician." Then it happened, when the musician played, that the hand of the LORD came upon him. ¹⁶And he said, "Thus says the LORD: "Make this valley full of ditches." 2 Kings 3.15-16

- **When a strong prophetic anointing descends.** Some people are unable to prophesy at any other time except when the special prophetic anointing descends upon them; it gives them the ability to do so. At other times, this might happen when

anointed prophets are present in the congregation. As the church worships and praises
God, His powerful prophetic anointing descends
upon it.

*"10When they came there to the hill, there was a group of
prophets to meet him; then the Spirit of God came upon
him, and he prophesied among them." I Samuel 10.10*

Worship music prepares the atmosphere for the
spirit of prophecy to descend and manifest itself in a
person or a church. When worship comes from the
heart, and when you learn to flow with the praise and
worship, the prophetic anointing is free to come
upon you. It is noteworthy to mention that the spirit
of prophecy descends occasionally, and it is not
something that is experienced all the time.

Conclusion

You have learned that there are five methods used to
prophesy. They are the gift of the prophet, the gift of
prophecy, the prophetic presbytery, the prophetic
preaching and the spirit of prophecy. The Lord
wants to comfort, edify and encourage His church
through these five methods.

CHAPTER VI

Prophetic Declaration and Decrees

ow you will learn what prophetic declarations and decrees mean and what they consist of. You might hear about them, but have no clear understanding of what they are or what their purpose is.

What is a prophetic declaration?

It is to declare or to speak a word coming from God. Sometimes this might include making future predictions.

What is a prophetic decree?

The prophetic decree prepares the way for God to do His job, as in the case of John the Baptist. In essence, the prophetic decree opens the way for God to do something. It doesn't give God freedom to act because He can't be bound, but it does activate God's power allowing Him to do what He wants to do. In other words, a prophetic decree gives God legal rights to do something here on earth. God is all powerful and He has chosen to use men to cooperate with him, not because He needs man, but because this is the way He decided it would be done.

Two ways to loosen God's power are:

- Our faith and obedience.
- Speaking and declaring His Word.

God is looking for men and women who dare to declare His Word. He is searching for mouths to speak the same words that He is saying.

What is a declaration or prophetic decree?

It is something that is **said or done** in the natural (the physical or earthly realm), but its effect takes place in the spiritual realm. Once the declaration or prophetic decree penetrates the spiritual realm, it returns producing change in the natural realm.

A declaration or a natural action	→	Affects or impacts the spiritual realm	→	Produces change in the natural realm

Biblical examples of declarations and prophetic decrees:

Prophetic decrees

- The bow and the arrows.

  "¹⁸Then he said, "Take the arrows"; so he took them. And he said to the king of Israel, "Strike the ground"; so he struck three times, and stopped. ¹⁹And the man of God was angry with him, and said, "You should have struck five or six times; then you would have struck Syria till you had destroyed it! But now you will strike Syria only three times." ²⁰Then Elisha died, and they buried him. And the raiding bands from Moab invaded the land in the spring of the year." 2 Kings 13.18-20

- Isaiah walked barefoot and naked for three years.

  "¹In the year that Tartan came to Ashdod, when Sargon the king of Assyria sent him, and he fought against Ashdod and took it, ²at the same time the LORD spoke by Isaiah the son

of Amoz, saying, "Go, and remove the sackcloth from your body, and take your sandals off your feet." And he did so, walking naked and barefoot." Isaiah 20.1-2

This symbolized that Egypt and Ethiopia were in Assyria's hands.

- Moses raised the rod.

  "15And the LORD said to Moses, "Why do you cry to Me? Tell the children of Israel to go forward. 16But lift up your rod, and stretch out your hand over the sea and divide it. And the children of Israel shall go on dry ground through the midst of the sea." Exodus 14.15-16

  "21Then Moses stretched out his hand over the sea; and the LORD caused the sea to go back by a strong east wind all that night, and made the sea into dry land, and the waters were divided. 22So the children of Israel went into the midst of the sea on the dry ground, and the waters were a wall to them on their right hand and on their left." Exodus 14.21-22

  "26Then the LORD said to Moses, "Stretch out your hand over the sea, that the waters may come back upon the Egyptians, on their chariots, and on their horsemen." Exodus 14.26

Prophetic declarations

"Again He said to me, "Prophesy to these bones, and say to them, "O dry bones, hear the word of the LORD!" Ezekiel 37.4

- In this verse, Ezekiel prophesizes to dry bones and to the wind.

- Declare a thing or a word and it will be established.

"28You will also declare a thing, and it will be established for you; so light will shine on your ways." Job 22.28

- Declare words in worship.

"6Let the saints be joyful in glory; let them sing aloud on their beds. 6Let the high praises of God be in their mouth, and a two-edged sword in their hand, 7to execute vengeance on the nations, and punishments on the peoples; 8to bind their kings with chains, and their nobles with fetters of iron; 9to execute on them the written judgment-- This honor have all His saints." Psalms 149.5-9

Where are these declarations and prophetic decrees coming from?

- They must be actions and words ordained by God.

"12Then the LORD said to me, 'You have seen well, for I am ready to perform My word'." Jeremiah 1.12

"1Therefore, holy brethren, partakers of the heavenly calling, consider the Apostle and High Priest of our confession, Christ Jesus." Hebrews 3.1

The word **confession** in the Greek language is *"homologeo,"* meaning to say the same thing. God is looking for people willing to open their mouths and declare what He is saying. He wants to do His will through people willing to declare it.

There are three things that you must do to confess and declare what God is saying:

- You must allow God to use you
- You must be in total agreement with Him

OUR VISION

The objective of our mission is to spiritually feed God's people through preaching and teaching and to take the Word of God everywhere it is needed.

LEADERS THAT CONQUER

Guillermo Maldonado
ISBN: 1-59272-023-4*

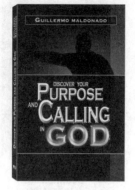

DISCOVER YOUR PURPOSE AND CALLING IN GOD

Guillermo Maldonado
ISBN: 1-59272-019-6

FORGIVENESS

Guillermo Maldonado
ISBN: 188392717-X*

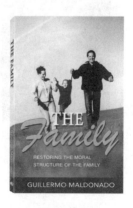

THE FAMILY

Guillermo Maldonado
ISBN: 1-59272-024-2

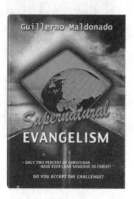

SUPERMATURAL EVANGELISM

Guillermo Maldonado
ISBN: 159272013-7

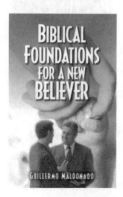

BIBLICAL FOUNDATIONS FOR A NEW BELIEVER

Guillermo Maldonado
ISBN: 1-59272-005-6

* Books available also in Spanish and French.

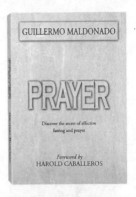

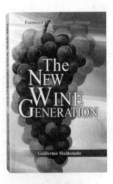
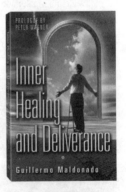
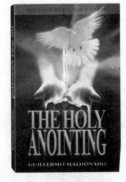